A LIFE IN THE WILD

PAMELA S. TURNER

A Life in the Wild

GEORGE SCHALLER'S STRUGGLE
TO SAVE THE LAST GREAT BEASTS

MELANIE KROUPA BOOKS
FARRAR, STRAUS AND GIROUX
NEW YORK

Text copyright © 2008 by Pamela S. Turner
Drawings and photographs copyright © 2008 by George B. Schaller
Maps copyright © 2008 by Jeffrey L. Ward
All rights reserved
Distributed in Canada by Douglas & McIntyre Ltd.
Printed in China by South China Printing Co. Ltd.
Designed by Jay Colvin
First edition, 2008
1   3   5   7   9   10   8   6   4   2

www.fsgkidsbooks.com

Library of Congress Cataloging-in-Publication Data
Turner, Pamela S.
    A life in the wild : George Schaller's struggle to save the last great beasts /
Pamela S. Turner.— 1st ed.
        p.   cm.
    ISBN-13: 978-0-374-34578-5
    ISBN-10: 0-374-34578-3
        1. Schaller, George B.— Juvenile literature.   2. Zoologists—United States—
Biography—Juvenile literature.   3. Wildlife conservation—Juvenile literature.
    I. Title.

QL31.S277T87 2008
590.92—dc22
[B]

2007042844

All drawings and photographs are courtesy of George B. Schaller and Kay M. Schaller
except for the following: pp. ii, 11, and 13, the Murie Center; p. 12, Jo Overholt; p. 16,
the American Museum of Natural History; pp. 26, 28, 33, and 89, Stan Wayman /
Time & Life Pictures / Getty Images; p. 86, Beth Wald; p. 88 (bear), Patrick Endres;
p. 88 (mountain gorilla) and p. 90 (lion), Pamela S. Turner.

To Lynne, in fond remembrance of our African adventures
—P.S.T.

Contents

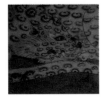

A LIFE IN THE WILD

The human species emerged enacting, dreaming, and thinking animals and cannot be fully itself without them.
—*Paul Shepard*

Prologue

Central India, 1964

THE COPPER SUN BURNED THROUGH A HAZY SKY. In the meadow dozens of barasingha deer crowded beneath a single tree, fanning their ears and jostling for a share of the shade.

George Schaller sat quietly in the nearby forest. He leaned back against a boulder overlooking a cow carcass in the ravine below. The beast's hindquarters were partially eaten, and deep puncture wounds riddled its throat. Sometime last night the cow had died in the jaws of a tiger. Would the predator return to its prey?

Insects droned in the still air. Hours passed; dusk gathered and the forest cooled. A brittle leaf crackled behind George. He rose slowly and turned, peeking over the rock—and straight into the eyes of a tigress.

George and the cat stared at each other, animal to animal, two ambassadors from alien nations. The tigress's amber gaze was fearless—and intense. George thought of running but fought down the urge.

The tigress's thoughts were probably simple. Friend? Foe? Or food?

Chapter 1: The Call of the Wild

The United States, 1947–1957

As they packed to leave, George's mother told him: "We can't take much. Besides clothes, you may bring one special thing."

It was 1947. Fourteen-year-old George, his mother, and his five-year-old brother, Chris, were leaving Europe for America. In the aftermath of World War II, displaced people from all over the globe were seeking new homes.

What to bring? George's decision was easy. As a boy growing up in Germany, he had loved wandering through nearby forests with only birds, squirrels, and an occasional roe deer for company. He imagined himself an explorer like Sven Hedin, who wrote about the snowy Himalayas, the forbidding Tibetan Plateau, and other faraway lands. During his own expeditions George sometimes spotted birds' nests in the forest. He would scramble up—heights never bothered him—and carry home an egg cupped in his hands. By poking two small holes in his fragile prize, he could blow out the contents and keep the delicate shell.

The egg collection, George decided, was the one special thing that

George and his pet raven at the University of Alaska, Fairbanks, in 1952.

would go with him to America. George packed a starling's egg, plain and white; a clear blue egg with black speckles, courtesy of a song thrush; the grayish, brown-mottled egg of a house sparrow; a green, brown-sprinkled egg from a lesser gray shrike; a blue-green blackbird egg; and the biggest of all, a gray-marbled crow's egg. Inside a barrel-shaped wooden box, cradled in a nest of cotton, the eggs held all the colors of earth and sky and forest.

The Schaller family arrived in St. Louis, Missouri, in 1947. Though she had lived many years in Germany, George's mother was American. In Missouri the Schaller boys met their American aunt, uncle, and cousins.

George enrolled in an American high school and learned to speak English. He did well in biology and creative writing, but disliked math and was bored by physics; overall he was a mediocre student. After class he spent his time with his pets. He kept lizards, pigeons, an opossum, even a beautiful (but poisonous) copperhead snake.

When George was seventeen, his older cousin, Ed, who had briefly lived in Alaska, invited George to join him for a vacation in Ontario, Canada. George and Ed camped, canoed, and fished for pike. Moose waded through the shallows under brilliant skies crossed by bald eagles. George returned to Missouri, but he was determined to find his way back to those wild northern lands.

In his senior year of high school, George took an aptitude test to help him choose an occupation. The result? Interior decorator. George wisely ignored this advice and applied for admission to the University of Alaska, Fairbanks. Months passed without a response. Instead of abandoning his plans, George got on a plane. As he recalls, "I just showed up, paid my sixty-dollar fee, and they let me stay."

Fairbanks suited him. The university was small, and everyone received personal attention from the professors. George's favorite subject was zoology, especially animal behavior. By watching an animal closely and writing down observations, a scientist could begin to interpret *why* an animal behaved the way it did. How had the behavior evolved? What did the behavior say about the social life of the species? George also learned about

George, age six, in Dresden, Germany. It was traditional to give children a paper cone full of candy to celebrate their first day of school.

6

ecology: Which animals lived in which habitats? How did they interact with other animals, and with their environment?

To his delight, George was required to spend his summers doing field research. For his first summer project nineteen-year-old George, together with a fellow student, surveyed bird species along the remote Colville River in northern Alaska. As they canoed down the Colville, the two students spotted bluethroats, arctic terns, golden plovers, and willow warblers. Golden eagles, peregrine falcons, gyrfalcons, and rough-legged hawks nested among the riverside bluffs and cliffs.

George's companion, an experienced falconer, captured a fledgling gyrfalcon and tied it to his canoe. Soon the young bird was eating raw meat from his hand. Not to be outdone, George captured a young raven for *his* canoe. The raven became so tame he didn't need to be tied up at all.

This was the life George had loved since childhood: being with wild animals and exploring the natural world. As he later admitted, "Essentially, I never grew up."

When the bird survey was finished (62 species were recorded), George and his raven went back to the university. One of his classmates was Kay Morgan, a warm and lively young woman from Anchorage. Kay had grown up in central California and moved to Alaska as an adolescent. When she moved farther north to study anthropology and biology in Fairbanks, her family in Anchorage had teased her: "Watch out for the people up there! Some of them get 'arctic madness' and go crazy."

One day Kay was in her dorm room when she heard someone bellowing. Poking her head out the window, she saw a tall young man standing beside the dormitory, yelling and shaking his fist at the sky. Kay was shocked. There really *was* such a thing as arctic madness!

A flutter of black landed on the young man's wrist. He bent his head and spoke quietly to the raven. Kay was intrigued. She thought she recognized him from one of her classes: the serious student with a faint German accent.

After their next class she asked, "Was that *you* with the raven?" George confessed he was, indeed, the arctic madman. Shortly afterward the raven abandoned George to join a local raven gang. George and Kay became friends.

The raven wasn't George's only unusual pet. A friend gave him an orphaned woodchuck. George kept it in his dorm room until the woodchuck made itself unpopular by munching through the wall and into another student's room. George released his toothy friend in the woods that spring.

During his junior year at college, George learned of a scientific expedition to the remote Brooks Range in northeastern Alaska. Only the native Gwich'in and Inupiat peoples and a handful of explorers had ever set foot in the Brooks Range. It was America's last great wilderness.

The expedition would be headed by legendary biologist Olaus Murie and his wife, Mardy. The Muries were old-time Alaskans (their honeymoon was a 500-mile dogsled trip), but they had new ideas about wilderness conservation. George wrote to Olaus, who generously invited him along. The expedition was called off when Olaus Murie became ill, but Olaus didn't forget George.

George graduated from the University of Alaska in 1955 with degrees in zoology and anthropology. He also gave a small but special parting gift to the university's natural history collection: the box of bird eggs he'd brought to America from Germany.

At the suggestion of one of his professors, Brina Kessel, he applied to the University of Wisconsin for graduate school and was accepted. Kay Morgan also moved to Wisconsin. In 1957, she and George married.

At the University of Wisconsin, George studied under Professor John Emlen. "Doc," as everyone called Professor Emlen, was an ornithologist—a bird expert. Doc asked George to study a question in bird behavior: At what age do young birds show fear?

With Kay's help George hatched chicks, ducklings, and pheasants from eggs and visited the nests of robins and bluebirds around campus. As the baby birds grew, George periodically showed them different objects—such as colored pieces of cardboard and a rubber owl—and recorded their reactions. He found that there is an inborn fear response in birds. The timing varies by species, but at a definite age all young birds become afraid of strange objects.

George's favorite study animal was a young blue heron he hatched from an egg he collected by climbing high into an elm tree. At hatching, Siegfried—as George called him—was comically hideous. His gray down

was patchy and damp, and his gangly neck couldn't support his oversize head. But in just a few days Siegfried was sitting up and greedily snapping at the raw meat George offered him. Soon the young heron grew big enough to swallow dead fish and rats in one gulp. After meals Siegfried would sit in George's lap, stretching out his neck to rest his head on George's shoulder. If anyone else came near, Siegfried flapped his wings and roared furiously.

When his adopted bird-child was three months old, George took Siegfried to a nearby marsh to release him back into the wild. The spot was a heron's delight, full of reeds, frogs, and fish. Siegfried waded out and immediately began eyeing a school of minnows. His mind, as usual, was focused on his stomach.

"Good fishing, Siegfried," called George. He tried to walk away, but the heron flew over him, circled, and landed. George carried him back to the swamp. This time Siegfried stayed where he belonged—in the wild.

DURING HIS FIRST YEAR OF GRADUATE SCHOOL, George heard again from Olaus Murie. Olaus's health had recovered, and the expedition to the remote Brooks Range in northern Alaska was back on. Was George still interested? Yes, he was.

On a fine June morning in 1956, the expedition set off. George, now twenty-three, looked down in awe at the vast Sheenjek River valley from a small Cessna plane. To the north lay the raw, rugged peaks of the Brooks Range. Beyond the mountains spread the coastal plain where polar bears made dens and caribou gave birth. It was a land of unclimbed summits, unnamed lakes, and rivers that flowed into mystery.

A bush pilot flew George, the Muries, and two other scientists, Bob Krear and Brina Kessel (George's former professor), to a lake in the valley. As they set up camp, George pointed and shouted, "Grizzlies!" On the lake's opposite shore two tawny bears were playing a spirited game of catch-me-if-you-can.

During the exuberant Alaskan summer the landscape teemed with life. A pair of mew gulls nested in a spruce tree near the camp, dive-bombing anyone who came too close. White wildflowers powdered the meadows, and iridescent fish filled the icy streams. Even the rocks bloomed with orange and yellow lichens.

Expedition leader Olaus Murie hoped that by documenting this land's riches they might convince the government to protect it. Part of the process was scientific: How many species lived here, and in which habitats? Part of the process was educational: How could they best communicate the wonders of this pristine wilderness? The expedition members took notes, gathered specimens, and captured images on film.

As George explored, he found a patchwork of distinct habitats: the lakeshore, the tundra, the tundra pools, the woodlands along the streams, the spruce forests on the lower mountain slopes, and the alpine world at the summits. He recorded all the plants and animals living in each place.

Olaus encouraged George's wanderings. He believed a scientist should gather his or her data on foot, every sense alert, notebook and camera in hand. Olaus also helped George identify rare birds and taught him how to distinguish the droppings of different predators by their size, color, and shape. A predator's feces revealed what the predator had eaten, Olaus explained. A scientist might not see a wolf, fox, lynx, or grizzly bear kill its prey, but undigested bone and hair could still tell the story.

Brina Kessel, George, Don McLeod (a visiting friend of the Muries), Mardy Murie, and Olaus Murie in the Sheenjek River Valley.

George, Olaus, Mardy, Bob, and Brina gathered around the nightly campfire to share the discoveries of the day: a bold wolf trotting past camp, a bull moose ambling along the lakeshore, a nest of golden eaglets tucked into a limestone cliff.

Even after a full day of hiking and climbing, George glowed with excitement. "From the top, the mountains just go like this, up and down, up and down," George told his companions. "You want to keep going, up one ridge and down another."

Olaus nodded and smiled. Too often, he told them, scientists are obsessed with collecting facts. They forget that wilderness has spiritual value, that wild places feed the heart as well as the mind. As scientists, they all had a moral obligation to protect this wilderness so that others could immerse themselves in its peace and beauty.

Soon after, George departed on a weeklong solo trip to explore the headwaters of the Sheenjek River. He carried a sixty-pound backpack with food for ten days, a sleeping bag, an air mattress, and a tarp in case of rain.

George followed trails made by wild sheep and caribou. He climbed over a mountain pass as snow-white Dall sheep watched from their rocky perches. Hours later he hiked down to a river and laid his sleeping bag on the gravel bank. Too tired to cook, he pulled crackers and raisins from his pack, drank a cup of icy river water, and climbed into his sleeping bag.

Grunt-splash-crunch-splash.

George sat up with a start. A herd of caribou emerged from the pale morning light. The ground vibrated as hundreds of grunting animals—males, females, and clumsy calves—surrounded him and flowed along the banks and through the shallows like a great furry river. Heads and antlers nodding, wide feet plodding, the caribou paid him no attention at all.

He realized this must be part of the Porcupine herd, named for the Porcupine River. The herd migrated to the plains north of the Brooks Range every spring to calve. Now they were returning to their winter ranges in the south. George felt honored to witness this ancient trek.

George made many more solo trips that summer. By the beginning of August, his wanderings had worn out two pairs of boots and his observations filled five notebooks. Snow dusted the nearby peaks, and the willow leaves turned yellow. One day Bob Krear pointed out that it was strangely quiet near camp; the mew gull family had left.

Female caribou and calves fording a river in northern Alaska.

"I guess it's time for us to go, too," said George. "But how I hate to leave this country!"

The expedition flew south on August 5. In two months they had recorded 85 bird species and 18 species of mammals. They collected 138 species of flowering plants, 40 species of lichen, and dozens of insects. The team also took hundreds of photographs and enough film for a documentary. George wrote the expedition report, titled "Arctic Valley," and Olaus used it, along with the expedition's photos and film, to convince the U.S. government to protect this precious wilderness. In 1960 the area they had explored and studied became the Arctic National Wildlife Refuge, stretching over almost nine million acres.

"A good field worker must find joy in solitude, strong willpower in the face of discomfort, and a passion to be in the outdoors," says George.

For George, the Murie expedition was to become the model for the rest of his career: exploration, rigorous science, passionate conservation, and a deep, heartfelt connection to wild places and wild animals.

George rejoined Kay at the University of Wisconsin and finished his master's degree. One day, six months after returning from Alaska, George stopped by Doc Emlen's office. Doc leaned back in his chair and eyed George. *Hmmm,* thought Doc. *Earnest, hardworking, enthusiastic. Best of all, young enough to try something crazy.*

"Would you like to study gorillas?" Doc asked.

Chapter 2: Gorilla Forest

THE BELGIAN CONGO, CENTRAL AFRICA, 1959–1960

Then the underbrush swayed rapidly just ahead, and presently before us stood an immense male gorilla . . . And now truly he reminded me of nothing but some hellish dream creature . . . He advanced a few steps—then stopped to utter that hideous roar . . . Just as he began another of his roars, beating his breast in rage, we fired, and killed him.

With a groan which had something terribly human in it, and yet was full of brutishness, he fell forward on his face. The body shook convulsively for a few minutes, the limbs moved about in a struggling way, and then all was quiet—death had done its work, and I had leisure to examine the huge body.

—*Paul B. Du Chaillu*, Explorations and Adventures in Equatorial Africa, *1861*

The gorillas in Group 4 huddle behind their leader, Big Daddy.

In Du Chaillu's time, and for decades after, the study of exotic animals by Western scientists was often brutal: find it, kill it, examine the corpse. Scientists and collectors all over the globe sent lifeless birds stuffed with cotton, limp bundles of fur, and boxes of bones to Western museums and universities.

In 1959 twenty-six-year-old George Schaller began pioneering research on wild gorillas in Africa. His work would help transform the way scientists studied wildlife.

• • •

WHEN DOC EMLEN ASKED GEORGE if he'd like to study gorillas, George impulsively agreed. He then read everything about gorillas he could find, including Paul B. Du Chaillu's *Explorations and Adventures in Equatorial Africa*, written almost a hundred years before. George suspected that Du Chaillu's stories were exaggerated, but there was no denying the terrifying power of an angry gorilla. One of Du Chaillu's African companions had bled to death after being attacked during a gorilla hunt.

Later explorers confirmed the gorilla's ferocity, including Carl Akeley. The museum collector shot five gorillas in the Virunga Volcanoes of the Belgian Congo (now known as the Democratic Republic of the Congo) in 1921. Akeley later helped create Albert National Park (now called Virunga National Park) to protect gorillas. Yet he wrote: "The white man who will allow a gorilla to get within ten feet of him without shooting is a plain darn fool."

Could these elusive, possibly dangerous animals be studied in the wild? George Schaller and Doc Emlen were determined to try. They planned to begin with a six-month survey of gorilla habitat in the Belgian Congo, Rwanda, and Uganda. Doc and George would hike through forests looking for gorillas. Even if they didn't spot any actual gorillas, they could count fresh signs of gorillas such as droppings, nests, and feeding sites. A survey would answer some basic yet important questions about gorillas: How many were there? Where did they live? If observing wild gorillas really was possible, the survey would also help them select the best site for the project George hoped to take on: an intensive, yearlong study of gorilla behavior.

George and Kay Schaller and Doc Emlen and his wife, Jinny, traveled to Albert National Park in the Belgian Congo, where Carl Akeley had once hunted gorillas. The park was a cluster of jungle-covered volcanoes almost completely surrounded by African farms. Doc and George decided that the

Gorilla pelts are laid out to dry during Carl Akeley's 1921 expedition to the Virunga Volcanoes. The skinned body of a juvenile gorilla hangs from a tent pole.

two of them would hike to Kabara, a park ranger's cabin high in the mountains. From Kabara they would search for mountain gorillas, a subspecies found only in these cool, high-altitude forests.

A line of porters carried the scientists' supplies in bundles on their heads, just as in Du Chaillu's time. Doc and George were drenched in sweat and breathing heavily by the time they reached Kabara, at an altitude of 10,000 feet. The cabin stood in a flower-dotted meadow between two towering volcanic peaks. It was one of the loveliest spots George had ever seen.

Doc Emlen and the porters slept in the rough wooden cabin, but George preferred to spread his sleeping bag on cool grass under a star-sprinkled sky. He woke just as the sun capped the volcanoes. A forest duiker—a small antelope—stepped delicately into the meadow to graze the dewy grass. The fresh morning light gilded its fur a gleaming red-gold. With a glance toward George, the duiker fled back into the forest with high, nervous leaps.

Later that morning the scientists began their search for gorillas. Doc and George split up to cover as much ground as possible. During the first two days they found only gorilla nests—circles of leaves and branches that gorillas gather around them when they prepare to sleep. But on the third day, far in the distance, George heard the quick *pok-pok-pok* of a gorilla beating its chest. His own heart drummed *pok-pok-pok* in joy and excitement.

The next day Doc and George hiked to the spot where George had heard the chest-beating. They found a trampled path littered with pieces of wild celery and nettles—leftovers from an ape lunch. While Doc stayed behind to take notes, George tracked the gorillas. The animals had left a winding trail of crushed leaves and trampled vines; a musky-sweet gorilla smell lingered in the air. Then a roar sounded in the distance: *UUUA . . . UUUA!*

George felt the hairs on his neck rise. He took a few steps, stopped to listen, moved, and stopped again. Now there was no sound except the buzzing of insects. He scrambled over a ridge, through mists clinging to the lower slopes, and up again. Then he spotted them on the opposite hillside—great black beasts, some nestled in trees, others sitting on the ground.

A group of gorillas watches George from a moss-draped tree. One of the gorillas, a female, beats her chest in excitement.

George was stunned. Until this moment he had only seen zoo gorillas, dispirited animals with dull fur and blank expressions. These wild gorillas were magnificent creatures, glossy blue-black with glowing caramel eyes. One gorilla's back had the gray hair of a silverback, a full-grown male. The silverback spotted George, rose, and pounded his chest: *Pok-pok-pok.*

Although he had been face-to-face with other wild animals, George had never felt an urge to speak to one. This beast was different. By word or gesture George longed to say: *I mean you and your family no harm, I only want to be near you.* As man and ape stared at each other across the valley—and the greater void of time and evolution—George wondered if the gorilla also felt some faint sense of kinship.

18

The spell was broken by shouts from the forest: "George! George!" called Doc. He had become increasingly worried about George after hearing gorilla roars followed by silence. At the sound of Doc's voice, the gorillas fled.

The scientists tracked the gorillas and two hours later found the group again. The silverback roared when he spotted the two men, yet he quickly calmed down. Doc and George watched in wonder as a female sat next to the giant male and rested against his side. In one arm she held a small black bundle. It kicked its spindly legs and waved its tiny arms.

"It must have just been born," George whispered to Doc. "It's still wet."

The male gorilla—that beast of legendary ferocity—reached over and gently touched the baby.

Doc and George were elated. They had tracked gorillas and observed the animals behaving calmly and naturally. Studying wild gorillas *was* possible!

Over the next few months the two scientists traveled to many other forests in the Belgian Congo, Rwanda, and Uganda to count gorillas, learn more about their habitat, and find the most promising site for George's long-term study of gorilla behavior. Sometimes the work was dangerous— but not because of savage gorillas.

George was hiking through a bamboo forest near Mount Tshiaberimu when he noticed a lone vine stretched conspicuously across the path. *Odd,* thought George. He paused to look around. Everything seemed normal. He looked up to discover a six-foot log with an iron spear in the end. Suspended twenty feet above, it pointed directly at George's head. It was an elephant trap set by poachers. Had George blundered into the vine, it would have unleashed the spear-tipped log, heavy enough to impale a five-ton elephant.

COUNTING WILD GORILLAS proved to be very difficult because the animals were constantly on the move. However, Doc and George were able to estimate that 3,000 to 15,000 eastern lowland gorillas lived in central Africa. The mountain gorilla subspecies was much rarer—they estimated that there were only about 450 in the Virunga Volcanoes. But the mountain gorillas lived in a relatively small area, so the Virungas had twice as many gorillas per square mile as any other region. It would be the best site for George's in-depth study.

A detailed study meant spending as much time as possible with gorillas, carefully gathering and analyzing thousands of small details about their food habits, sounds, movements, temperaments, daily routines, and social interactions. It would mean living in a remote, ramshackle cabin with no plumbing or electricity for at least a year. But George was excited by the idea of immersing himself in the gorillas' world. As George put it, he sought "not just to know the species but to understand it, slowly unfolding its life like an origami."

Doc and his wife returned to Wisconsin while George and Kay moved to the cabin at Kabara to become neighbors of the mountain gorillas. Fifty-five porters trudged up to Kabara with the Schallers' supplies: cases of canned meats, fruits, and vegetables; sacks of flour and potatoes; a basket of live chickens for laying fresh eggs; heavy clothing; bedding; rain gear; books; and a first-aid box. George and Kay nailed grass mats and colorful African cloth to the cabin walls to keep out the drafts, and sorted the mountain of bags, duffels, and boxes. At last they were unpacked, and George's gorilla study could finally begin.

Living in the human world requires blocking out much of the din and distraction going on around us. Living in the wild requires opening up every one of our senses, especially our sense of wonder. As George spent time in the gorilla forest, he began to notice its hidden jewels: a bright blue earthworm writhing among the vines, a black-billed turaco flashing its bloodred wings, the faint rustle of a wild pig.

George quickly became attuned to the musty gorilla scent lingering on a path, a faint footprint in damp ground, or the soft *uuuhh-uuuhh* of a contented gorilla. He patiently tracked the gorillas through the forest and sat quietly when he found them. Sometimes the gorillas fled when they saw George; sometimes they roared or beat their chests. Yet often they ignored this odd white ape with binoculars. Day after day the gorillas let George get closer. This gentle, step-by-step method of getting wild animals used to the presence of people is now called habituation.

One day George was crouched on a low-hanging tree branch when a young male gorilla spotted him. It beat its chest in alarm. The silverback of the group, whom George had named Mr. Crest, rattled the forest with a tremendous roar. But instead of running off, Mr. Crest and his group strode over and gathered under the branch George was sitting on. George didn't move, but his heart was pounding.

A female clutching an infant sidled toward George's branch, reached up, and gave it a sharp tug. He stayed very still. Suddenly, the gorilla swung onto the branch and perched next to George. She acted as if he wasn't there. George tried to act as if she wasn't there, either. Finally his anxiety turned to amusement. This was, he realized, a lot like two strangers awkwardly sharing a park bench. They sat side by side until the gorillas finally tired of George and moved off to feed.

During his yearlong study George discovered eleven gorilla groups and several lone males living around Kabara. Group 4 taught him the most. Its leader, Big Daddy, was the calmest silverback George observed. D.J. was second in command and reminded George of a young businessman hoping for a promotion. Another silverback, the Outsider, was the biggest gorilla George had ever seen. Although larger than Big Daddy, the Outsider never challenged him for leadership. Group 4 had only one blackback (a male not yet old enough to have silver hair). Junior, as George christened him, would often leave the other gorillas to rest near George. Group 4 also had ten adult females, including Mrs. Wrinkle, a sad-eyed gorilla with a face like a raisin.

Junior, a young male, struts along a log. Of all the gorillas, he seemed to take the most pleasure in being near George.

Once, George decided to spend the night with Group 4. He found them late in the day and observed them, unnoticed, from the bushes. Four infants turned a slanting tree into a slide, zipping down on their rumps or bellies, then scrambling one after another back up to the top.

A female came to the bottom of the tree, folded her arms, and looked pointedly at the youngsters. It was, George thought, as if she were saying: *Bedtime!* The playmates came down obediently. Yet they couldn't resist using the female as a jungle gym. The little gorillas leaped on her head, bounced down her back, and slid off her rump before scampering off into their mothers' waiting arms.

Big Daddy began grabbing nearby branches and shrubs and bending them under his body. Taking the hint, the other gorillas built night nests of their own. One infant made a nest in a tree, but after a few minutes he decided that cuddling with his warm, furry mother was a better idea.

George reviews his field notes inside the cabin at Kabara.

Rain drizzled down on the silent black hulks of the gorillas. George laid his sleeping bag beneath a sloping tree about forty yards from the gorillas and ate a dinner of crackers and canned sardines. Soon he was sleeping as soundly as Big Daddy.

WHEN GEORGE WASN'T IN THE FOREST, he was at Kabara with Kay. George organized his notes while Kay used their cranky woodstove to dry samples of the plants gorillas ate. Although the Schallers were often alone, they were never lonely. A pair of duikers courted in the meadow, and a forest buffalo lumbered up nightly to rub his hide against the cabin wall. Every morning at sunrise, George and Kay were awakened by two white-necked ravens. The birds enjoyed crash-landing on the hut's metal roof and sliding down with a nail-scraping *screeeeeech*. Kay loved the ravens. Clever, curious, and mischievous, they were like monkeys with wings. She fed them scraps, and when she cawed the pair flew down to perch on her arm.

Once, George was in the forest watching gorillas and eating lunch when he noticed the ravens flying high above. When they spotted George, they spiraled down, causing the silverback to jump up and roar in alarm while the female gorillas screamed. The birds gleefully dive-bombed the terrified gorillas until they finally tired of ape torture and landed to claim the remains of George's lunch.

As he observed the gorillas day after day, George was struck by the parallels between gorillas and humans. When angry, excited, or afraid, the gorillas would beat their chests and throw vegetation. George realized this was "displacement behavior"—a way of releasing tension used by many species, including humans. The gorillas were like people slamming doors during an argument or yelling and stomping during football games.

There were times when the gorillas' resemblance to humans was almost too painful to watch. One day Mrs. Wrinkle emerged from the bushes with a newborn baby. She held her little one gently and gazed at it tenderly. Two days later George saw Mrs. Wrinkle again, but this time the infant lay limp in her arms. Day after day Mrs. Wrinkle carried her dead baby. She no longer held it close to her chest, yet she refused to abandon it. Finally, four days after its death, Mrs. Wrinkle left her infant facedown on the trail.

The skeleton of a newborn gorilla would be of scientific interest, so George carefully carried the fragile body back to Kabara. As he stripped the skin and muscle from the bones of the little baby, so much like a human infant, he felt sad.

Kay watches Mr. Crest and two other gorillas. She sometimes joined George in the forest, but the gorillas were more nervous around two people.

Yet even this unhappy event helped George understand the mountain gorillas. By counting gorilla births and deaths, George estimated how many young gorillas survive to adulthood (only about half). He was also able to calculate how fast a gorilla population can grow. The answer: very slowly. Females usually have only one infant at a time, and births are spaced three to four years apart. George knew this low reproductive rate made gorillas extremely vulnerable to extinction.

Through 466 patient hours of observation, George documented the leisurely lives of gorillas. He recorded their sounds and interpreted their meanings: the grunt of annoyance, the chuckle of playtime, the bark of alarm and warning. George studied the forest ecosystem and recorded what the gorillas ate (at least 100 species of plants). He gave gorilla foods a taste test: some reminded him of radishes, while others were spit-it-out-quick bitter. He mapped the movements of the different gorilla groups and found that they wandered freely within their range, but did not defend a territory, as scientists had previously believed. George even studied handedness in gorillas by recording which hand a gorilla used first when chest-beating (the right hand was used first 81 percent of the time). Did a preference for using the right hand evolve long ago, perhaps in a common ancestor of both gorillas and humans?

George also documented how gorillas of different sexes and ages treated each other. His study revealed that gorillas were calm, social creatures. Even when strange males crossed paths, they preferred dramatic chest-beating and branch-throwing to real violence. The gorilla was never the savage brute of legend; people had wrongly projected their own dark fantasies onto another creature.

At first George worried he would not be able to tell the gorillas apart. He and his professor, John "Doc" Emlen, soon realized that every animal had a distinctive "nose print." By sketching these nose wrinkles George could identify each of the 169 gorillas in his study area.

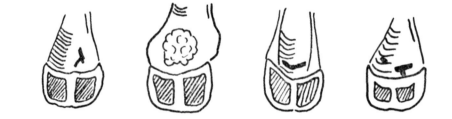

George's work had an impact far beyond the study of gorillas. He helped revolutionize field biology by showing that a supposedly dangerous animal could be observed in the wild with minimal risk. Patience and respect made all the difference. Many other scientists were inspired by George's research, and his techniques were eventually used to study animals ranging from orangutans to hammerhead sharks.

In 1960, political unrest in the Congo made the Virunga Volcanoes unsafe for the Schallers. It was hard to leave Kabara, with its idyllic meadow and impish ravens. Most of all, it was hard to leave the gorillas. For a year George had been with them almost every day.

As George and Kay prepared to go, the gorillas of Group 6 ambled to a slope behind the cabin. A female gorilla George had named Mrs. October was holding her eight-month-old infant. George was shocked to see that the baby had a bone-deep wound, bloody and ragged, on its rump. Mrs. October cared for her baby tenderly. She held the infant so the wound didn't touch her body, and she wouldn't let the other gorillas near her injured youngster.

George sketched gorilla mothers and infants in his field notes.

A week later George saw Mrs. October and her infant for the last time. The wound was crusted over, and the infant seemed stronger.

The next day the porters arrived to carry the Schallers' belongings down the mountain. George and Kay reluctantly followed. They never knew what happened to the little gorilla. They did know that the balance between life and death, for one baby or an entire species, can tip all too easily either way.

CHINA
PAKISTAN · New Delhi ★
NEPAL
KANHA
NATIONAL PARK
□
INDIA

0 Miles   1000
0 Kilometers 1000

Chapter 3: A Clan of Tigers

CENTRAL INDIA, 1963–1965

Just 150 years ago, countless deer, antelope, and wild cattle roamed India. The country was home to Earth's greatest congregation of carnivores: cheetahs, hyenas, wolves, wild dogs, leopards, lions, and the biggest of all big cats, the tiger. In one century (1860 to 1960), habitat destruction, disease, and hunting reduced India's spectacular wildlife to scattered remnants. By 1960, only a few thousand tigers remained.

In 1963, Kanha National Park was considered the finest reserve in India. Rudyard Kipling had chosen the area as the setting for *The Jungle Book*, his famous story about the wolf-boy Mowgli and the evil tiger Shere Khan, "The Striped One that comes by night."

India's tigers were legendary, yet there was little scientific knowledge about the great cats. At Kanha, George Schaller hoped to conduct the first detailed study of tigers and their prey. What could be learned about the secretive lives of tigers? What effect did this hunter have on the creatures it hunted?

A resting tiger in Kanha National Park.

George was now thirty years old, with a Ph.D. in zoology from the University of Wisconsin. He was also a father. George and Kay had two sons, two-and-a-half-year-old Eric and one-year-old Mark. They settled into a small bungalow in Kanha National Park to begin family life in the wild.

• • •

A WARNING CAME FROM THE RAVINE: a deep, rumbling growl.

George froze. The hidden tiger was probably guarding a kill. He made a prudent detour but later returned to find a dead gaur bull (the gaur is a species of wild cattle) at the bottom of the ravine. Or, rather, half a gaur—apparently rump steak was a feline favorite. George crouched behind a tree and waited.

A female tiger and her large cub in Kanha.

A tigress wove silently toward the kill, her striped coat making her almost invisible amid the light-and-dark mosaic of the forest. As she stepped out and stood over the dead gaur, George noticed a notch missing from her left ear. Cut-Ear, as George dubbed her, bit a strip of flesh from the carcass and gulped it down. Four cubs, about four months old, tumbled out of the underbrush and pounced enthusiastically on the carcass. One grabbed a piece of skin and jerked it ferociously back and forth.

When her belly was full, Cut-Ear grunted softly and walked to a grassy slope. The cubs fell in line behind her like a flock of ducklings. Cut-Ear flopped down. One cub climbed a sapling while another stalked an insect through the dry grass. The third cub crouched and ambushed the fourth. The two rolled and tumbled together like a fuzzy black-and-orange basketball.

Four healthy cubs was a big litter; George knew it would become in-creasingly difficult for Cut-Ear to feed them all as they grew. He wondered: How many of this tiger clan would survive?

Kanha National Park was a graceful land of rolling hills, forested ravines, and tree-dotted meadows. The Schallers' small house was right in the middle of George's study area—twenty square miles in the center of the park. Eric and Mark played in their bamboo-fenced yard under Kay's watchful eye; sometimes she took the boys for rides perched on the back of the park's elephant. George spent his days driving Kanha's roads and

Kay, Eric, and Mark go looking for tigers.

29

hiking—alone and unarmed—beside forest streams and along ravines, always alert for tiger signs: a roar, paw prints in the mud, or the pungent scent marks tigers spray to announce their presence to other tigers. Finding a tiger kill, however, was always the best way for George to find a tiger. Even when not eating, tigers often lounged nearby.

A tigress sprays scent mark on grass, a pungent message that says *I was here* to other tigers. George could smell a fresh tiger scent mark from several yards away.

One day George found a half-eaten cow in a ravine and sat down to wait for the tiger to return. It was the dry season, and the forest was brown and brittle. All was quiet except for humming insects. George sat with his back against a boulder at the top of a ridge, looking down on the carcass. Several hours passed. Then he heard the faint rustling of a leaf behind him. He slowly peeked over the rock and found himself looking straight into Cut-Ear's eyes. Her white-fringed face was just a few feet away. George wanted to run, but instead he forced himself to stay as still as possible. Finally, Cut-Ear turned and walked off, casting one cool glance back at George.

Most tiger sightings were not so heart-stopping, but mapping each one helped George understand how far Kanha's tigers ranged and how much space they needed. It was vital information for tiger conservation. George discovered four adult tigers living in his study area: Cut-Ear, two other tigresses, and a large male. He could recognize each by their size and the distinctive stripe patterns on their faces. Tigers were supposed to be loners. George wondered what happened when Kanha's tigers crossed paths. Did they fight?

To understand Kanha's tigers, George also needed to study the antelope, deer, and wild cattle they hunted. Blackbuck antelopes, with their striking black-and-white coats and long spiral horns, were the most beautiful of Kanha's hoofed animals. The most common were the delicate chital deer (also called axis deer), which looked like overgrown fawns with their tawny, white-spotted coats. The rarest hoofed animal was the large, graceful barasingha deer. Barasingha were almost as rare as tigers; there were only about seventy-five at Kanha and just a few thousand left in all of India.

Blackbuck, chital, and barasingha were often seen in the meadows. In the forests lived the shy sambar deer. When sambar sensed danger, they gave a barklike alarm call that echoed through the forest, alerting George to the presence of tigers.

Gaur were the largest animals in Kanha. Gaur bulls sometimes intimidated each other by standing parallel, heads lowered and backs hunched, as if to say, *Check me out, I'm bigger than you.* The smaller bull always turned aside in submission.

Once, when George was watching a gaur herd, a bull sidled up and gave the hunchback display to George's Land Rover. George drove parallel to the bull. After sizing up the automotive competition, the gaur turned submissively away. *I won!* George thought, amused.

As the hot season wore on, George saw Cut-Ear's family often. One day he found Cut-Ear and her six-month-old cubs resting near a chital kill. The tigress rolled lazily onto her back, all four paws dangling comically in the air. A cub walked up to Cut-Ear, held her head between its paws and licked its mother's face. Cut-Ear purred.

In late June the weather cooled and waves of rain clouds drenched the dry land. George marveled as Kanha was transformed from brittle brown to fleshy green. Frogs croaked, winged termites swarmed, and wild orchids burst from the forest floor. Newborn blackbuck, sambar, and barasingha fawns toddled after their mothers.

To understand what effect tigers had on Kanha's hoofed animals, George needed to know: What does a tiger eat? How often does it kill? Unfortunately, Cut-Ear and the other tigers usually hid the carcasses of their prey by dragging them into thick brush. So he turned to the technique Olaus Murie had taught him in Alaska. George gathered tiger feces and looked carefully at the undigested hair inside. The hairs of most Kanha prey species were so different that George could immediately tell which animal had been the tiger's meal.

After examining hundreds of tiger feces, he concluded that chital made up half of all tiger prey at Kanha. A combination of sambar, barasingha, and gaur made up another fourth. About 10 percent of tiger prey consisted of domestic animals taken from local villages—a dangerous situation for both people and tigers.

Sometimes George was able to observe a tiger making a kill from a game-watching blind the park rangers had built in a meadow near the Schallers' bungalow. One day, as Eric and Mark stayed home with a babysitter, Kay joined George in the blind. Together they witnessed a tiger attack on a domestic buffalo.

Cut-Ear rose like a ghost from the grass and rushed the buffalo from behind, grabbing its hind leg and pulling with such force that the beast collapsed. As soon as it was down, she expertly darted past its flailing hooves and seized its throat. Suddenly the tigress let go, vaulted onto the buffalo's back, and grabbed its throat again, jerking the buffalo's head back with such force that George and Kay heard the neck snap from eighty feet away.

After snacking on the buffalo's rump, Cut-Ear left to fetch her cubs. Soon the quartet bounded out of the bushes. The nine-month-old cubs were now the size of Saint Bernard dogs. The largest cub, a male, took the prime spot at the rump, roaring at a sister when she tried to crowd in. Sister jumped back. Clearly, the largest cub had priority at a kill. *If there isn't enough food for all,* George realized, *the smaller cubs die.*

Cut-Ear returned, followed by a huge male tiger with a scraggly ruff around his face. George had often seen this fellow padding along the park roads. The cubs bounded up to greet Cut-Ear and the male, rubbing their heads affectionately against the adults' throats. Was this male the cubs' father? George thought so. It seemed that the supposedly solitary tiger was more family-oriented than anyone had suspected.

Cut-Ear and her three female cubs at a nighttime buffalo feast.

George and Kay watched the four cubs gorge themselves on the dead buffalo. Cut-Ear and the amiable male waited patiently for the cubs to eat their fill. Then Kay suddenly remembered that Eric and Mark were waiting for their own lunch. "I have to go back," she whispered to George.

"You'll have to walk home alone," murmured George, who was carefully timing how long each tiger spent eating.

By now the tigers were accustomed to seeing George walking around the park. Kay, however, wasn't used to strolling past bone-crunching, blood-lapping predators. She stood up straight and tall, not wanting George to know she was frightened.

"Kay?" George called softly as she left.

"Yes, George?"

"Bend down. Don't scare the tigers!"

Kay walked back home shaking her head. The tigers kept right on eating.

October brought the last of the rains and the beginning of the birth season for the chital and gaur. Although Cut-Ear caught the slower, more unwary calves and fawns, she still couldn't kill enough to feed her ravenous cubs. In desperation the tigress preyed on livestock in villages inside the park and along its borders. So did the eleven-month-old male cub, now almost as big as Cut-Ear. One night he snatched a squealing pig. It was the first time, to George's knowledge, that one of Cut-Ear's cubs had hunted for itself. Another night the male cub raided the Schallers' chicken coop and gobbled down all four hens.

The three female cubs were far less skilled than their brother. Once, George saw them attack a domestic buffalo. The cubs made several inept runs, but the buffalo snorted and charged, scattering the cubs. Then Cut-Ear appeared and quickly pulled the buffalo down. However, instead of grabbing its throat, Cut-Ear stood back. Her inexperienced cubs bit and clawed but didn't seem to understand how to deliver the final blow. Twice the buffalo shook off the cubs and rose to its feet. Twice more Cut-Ear knocked him down.

Two more tigers arrived—a tigress and a large cub. The cub joined the biting, clawing melee. When the youngsters finally dispatched the buffalo, all six tigers fed on the carcass. The two adult tigresses spent most of the time snarling at each other. Yet they didn't fight, and once again George was impressed by the tiger's sociability.

One night in December, George and Kay awoke to a ruckus coming from their shed, where they kept a domestic buffalo and a lamb they were fattening for Christmas dinner. A hole had been clawed through the shed's bamboo wall; the buffalo was dead and the lamb was gone. Apparently when the tiger realized it couldn't drag the buffalo through the hole, it grabbed the lamb instead.

George saw this as a perfect tiger-watching opportunity. He used the Land Rover to drag the dead buffalo away from their bungalow and tied the carcass to a stump.

Cut-Ear promptly showed up with her three hungry daughters. The Schallers' lamb had only been an appetizer. George watched the tiger family make a fine feast of the Schaller family buffalo. A few weeks later, on Christmas Day, the Schallers ate a dinner of canned ham instead of fresh lamb.

DURING HIS FOURTEEN MONTHS AT KANHA, George spent 129 hours observing tigers and almost 700 hours observing their prey. He counted the hoofed animals, watched what they ate, and noted how they behaved. George found that each species of hoofed animal lived off a slightly different part of the habitat: blackbuck ate meadow grass, chital ate the grasses along the forest border, and barasingha ate the dry ravine grasses. Sambar browsed in the forest, while gaur ate the coarsest grasses and the leaves of saplings.

In those days many people thought the numbers of predators should be controlled—even in national parks—so that herds of hoofed animals could grow faster. But George carefully counted each prey species at Kanha, the number of young born every year, and the number eaten by Kanha's tigers. He found that the tigers were good for the hoofed animals; by preying on the plant-eaters, the tigers helped keep the herds at a level the ecosystem could support. And the number of hoofed animals, in turn, determined how many tigers could live there.

Unfortunately, humans could upset this balance. George discovered that some parts of Kanha were overgrazed by domestic cattle, leaving less food for wildlife. Poachers were killing hoofed animals, too. Overgrazing and overhunting meant less prey for tigers, and without enough wild prey the tigers turned to domestic animals.

George's work also showed that tigers were not the bloodthirsty creatures of legend. They were even-tempered beasts, usually tolerant of humans and one another. Kanha's tigers had rewarded George's patience and persistence with intimate glimpses into their lives.

BY MARCH THE HOT SEASON HAD RETURNED and George's study was coming to a close. The cubs were now sixteen months old. The male cub could hunt as well as Cut-Ear, though the three female cubs were still getting help from their mother. George suspected that the three sisters would soon be completely independent.

The Schaller boys were growing, too. "Playing Daddy" became one of Eric and Mark's favorite games. They marched around the bungalow's bamboo-fenced yard, cupping their hands around their eyes to make pretend binoculars and peering into the bushes at pretend tigers and pretend deer. To George and Kay's great amusement, the little boys collected dirt clods and picked them apart with sticks—just as their dad picked apart tiger feces.

Eric and Mark take a bath in a plastic tub on the porch of the Schallers' Indian bungalow.

Three days before the Schallers left Kanha, George went for a walk in the forest. He passed a big rock without noticing the large female cub draped on top.

The tiger's head popped up. George found his face just a few feet from hers; she gave a growling roar as George backed away. The young tigress jumped down and bounded toward him. George scrambled up a tree; the cub halted, lay down nearby, and gazed up curiously.

Ten minutes later her brother arrived. The male cub lay down, too, oblivious to George. "Hello, there," George called down.

The bewildered cub looked right, left, forward, and behind. Finally he looked up at George, growled, and stalked disdainfully away. But the female cub remained and was soon joined by her sisters. All three seemed to enjoy

George-watching. It was only fair, considering all the time he'd spent staring at *them*.

George eventually got tired of the attention. "Go on!" he shouted. The three sisters jumped up and scampered off.

He thought back to his first sight of these cubs: so small, so charming, and so vulnerable. Life could be hard for tigers. It gave George great pleasure to know that Cut-Ear's clan had beaten the odds.

Chapter 4: Lion Country

TANZANIA, EAST AFRICA, 1966–1969

Even after India's wildlife was decimated, immense herds of animals remained in Africa. Africa's great beasts were saved by one of the slightest of creatures, the tsetse fly. For thousands of years this disease-carrying insect discouraged people from settling the savannahs and turning the wilderness into farmland.

After learning of George Schaller's successful tiger study, the head of Tanzania's national parks invited him to research predator–prey relations in the Serengeti. The complexity was daunting. In Serengeti National Park five major carnivores (lion, leopard, cheetah, hyena, and wild dog) pursued twenty different species of hoofed animals. How did this intricate ecosystem work?

In 1966 the Schaller family, including five-year-old Eric and three-and-a-half-year-old Mark, moved to a bungalow at Seronera in the middle of the Serengeti. Here, as nowhere else, George felt the pull of human prehistory. "Our dual past haunts us," George wrote. "We hear a lion roar and the pri-

A Serengeti lion at a kill.

mate in us shivers; we see huge herds of game and the predator in us is delighted, as if our existence still depended on their presence."

• • •

GEORGE AIMED AND FIRED. With a *spifft* the syringe shot out of the dart gun and into the lioness's flank. She twisted around, puzzled. George waited.

The young lioness lay down in the grass as the drug took effect. The other members of her pride ignored George's Land Rover; they saw it often. George drove behind the lioness's back. He stepped out quietly and knelt beside the motionless animal. There wasn't much time—the drug would not keep her asleep very long. Still, he couldn't resist the urge to run his hand across the cat's tawny fur.

George prepares to ear-tag a sedated lion.

George pulled out a plastic tag and quickly clamped it to the lioness's ear. These numbered tags were necessary because there were hundreds of lions in his study area around Seronera. Though he recognized many individual lions on sight, the tags would help him keep track of the rest, including this lioness.

George glanced at the lioness's rib cage. It was hardly moving. He had used the same dose of the drug on many lions, but this time something had gone wrong. *Accidentally killing a lion—my worst nightmare,* thought George. He grabbed the lioness's foreleg and pumped it up and down, compressing her broad chest, forcing air into her lungs.

A rumbling growl caught George by surprise. He looked up to see another lioness charging straight at him, her eyes full of fire. He dived into the Land Rover just as the lioness slid to a stop, snarling. George looked down at her, his heart pounding.

At least now the drugged lioness's heart was pounding, too. Her chest was rising and falling and in a few minutes she was looking around groggily. George felt weak with relief.

Though George preferred being on foot in the wilderness, the Land Rover had its uses. Besides being a haven from irritable lions, the car was a mobile observation station for George as he drove through the park's vast plains and scrubby woodlands on the lookout for lions, leopards, cheetahs, hyenas, and wild dogs.

On his second day in the Serengeti, he was driving along the edge of the plains when he spotted two lionesses. Their eyes were locked with laser-beam intensity on a herd of Thomson's gazelles walking single file. The lionesses melted into the golden grass, positioning themselves on either side of the approaching herd. The crouching cats were as still as death. George felt entwined in the lionesses' tension, poised on the knife edge of violence.

A breeze stirred. Lion scent filled the gazelles' nostrils and they exploded in panic. One gazelle ran straight at one of the hidden lionesses, recognizing the cat's muscular body only at the last moment. The desperate gazelle leaped high in the air. Two paws, with razored claws extended, shot out of the grass and snatched the gazelle from the sky. George was stunned, humbled, and thrilled. Such power and grace!

Witnessing kills was an essential part of George's research. He needed to know which predator had killed its own food and which was eating somebody else's dinner. Lions and hyenas often stole carcasses from each other, and hyenas stole from wild dogs. Both lions and hyenas stole from leopards, and everybody stole from cheetahs.

A lioness feeds on her kill, a topi antelope.

The wistful, elegant cheetahs were favorites of Kay's. When George stayed home with Eric and Mark, Kay drove off in search of the long-limbed cats. To her delight they sometimes jumped on the hood of the Land Rover to scan the horizon for prey. Their hunts were electrifying. A cheetah would trot toward a gazelle herd, then explode into action, rocketing after a zigzagging gazelle like a heat-seeking missile.

One female cheetah raised two cubs near Seronera, and George and Kay grew to know her well. They heard the mother cheetah call her cubs with chirps and chirrs, sounding more like a bird than a cat. When the cubs were half-grown, Kay saw the mother cheetah bring her daughters a live gazelle fawn. The

This female cheetah raised her cubs near the Schallers' home. One of the three cubs disappeared, but two lived to adulthood.

cubs needed to learn the family business: chase, knock down, grab by the throat, and hold until dead. After several inept tries the cubs managed to knock the fawn down, but their mother had to handle the killing.

The cheetah family left with the migrating gazelle herds. A year later George and Kay were delighted to see all three return; the two cubs were now almost full grown. One day as George was hiking on the plains, he spotted one of the sisters resting in the grass. George sat down nearby. She ignored him with the air of a princess.

A gazelle fawn bleated. George and the cheetah jerked to attention. The fawn appeared over a rise, two jackals nipping at its heels. The cheetah sprinted past George, knocked the fawn down, and seized its throat. The young cat had learned her lessons well.

She carried the fawn to a nearby waterhole while the jackals slunk away, disappointed. As the cheetah ate, George moved slowly closer . . . first on his hands and knees . . . then on his stomach. She glanced up but kept on eating. Twenty feet, fifteen feet, ten. George lay quietly in the grass next to the cheetah for over an hour. It was the kind of moment he treasured above all—no heart-pumping action, no thrill of fear, just the delight of a wild animal's generous acceptance.

George shows Mark and Eric how to blow out an ostrich egg he found abandoned in the Serengeti.

NONE OF THE SCHALLERS had to go far to see wildlife. Playful lions turned on the hose tap outside their house, gazelles grazed on the herbs in Kay's garden, and elephants toppled trees in the yard. White-necked ravens shadowed the sky, bringing happy memories of Kabara and the mountain gorillas.

Eric was now old enough for school, so Kay became his teacher while Mark played nearby. Sometimes their lessons and games were interrupted when an enormous belly filled the window. It was a bull giraffe (whom neighbors had named George, before the Schallers arrived), nibbling on the acacia tree beside the Schallers' house. George the giraffe liked to walk in his stately way through their clothesline, snapping the rope and dragging the laundry across the grass. George the scientist never minded cleaning up after him. The whole family was delighted to share their home with such a majestic beast.

Kay wasn't as thrilled with other visitors. George often brought home rotting skulls and tossed them onto the garage roof, safely away from hyenas, until he had time to clean and examine them. By checking the size of the skull, the presence or absence of horns, and the amount of wear on the teeth, George could estimate the age and sex of each species of prey animal taken by each kind of predator. But to Kay's wry amusement, this smelly science project attracted a ghoulish gathering of vultures and marabou storks. The Schaller garage looked perpetually decorated for Halloween.

The Serengeti's wild dogs were more welcome companions. One morning George was following a pack across the plains when one of the Land Rover's wheels became stuck in a warthog burrow. George got out to check for damage. When he looked up, he found himself surrounded by a semicircle of curious dogs. They were a comical sight with their patchwork coats, homely faces, and Mickey Mouse ears.

An adult wild dog and pups.

When the pack's interest waned, they trotted off; George jogged along several hundred feet behind. After trailing the pack for about a mile, he saw them run down and disembowel a zebra.

Hunters shot African wild dogs on sight because they thought the dogs' method of killing prey—ripping open the stomach—was cruel. (The cruelty of shooting the dogs was somehow overlooked.) Yet the more George learned about wild dogs, the more he admired them. They were canine Musketeers who lived the motto "all for one, and one for all." Wild dogs were devoted parents and always let pups eat first at a kill. Nobody was left out. Once George watched a dog with a withered leg arrive at a kill after all the food was gone. Another dog regurgitated meat for the lame dog to eat.

It troubled George that wild dogs were scarce in the park, even though prey was abundant and the dogs were protected from hunters. Why weren't there more wild dogs in the Serengeti?

His observations of one pack suggested an answer. George watched the dogs raise pups at a den in the plains. A few months later, the 34-dog pack appeared at Seronera near the Schallers' bungalow. Several dogs were sick. They staggered when they walked, and mucus ran from their eyes and mouths. Eight died within a week.

George captured a sick puppy and took it home. He hoped to have a vet examine it the next morning, but two hours later the pup whimpered feebly and died. When the vet examined the body, he discovered the pup had died from canine distemper, a disease of domestic dogs. Dogs living in villages near the park had transmitted the devastating illness to the wild dogs. Soon after, the surviving members of the wild dog pack left Seronera; George never saw them again.

George's main study animal in the Serengeti was not the sociable wild dog or the aloof cheetah, but the lion, the only cat that lives in groups. He discovered that a lion pride usually consists of related lionesses—mothers, daughters, grandmothers, aunts, and cousins—sharing a territory. Adult male lions—there are usually two to four in a pride—stay a few years until evicted by new males, who take over the pride and its territory. Lions living in prides won't tolerate strange lions of the same sex. Male pride lions will fight strange males, and pride lionesses will fight strange lionesses. There are also nomadic lions and lionesses that roam widely; the nomads don't defend a territory and are more tolerant of strange lions.

George wanted to know more about the daily lives of these nomadic lions. However, even with ear tags, nomads were difficult to locate day after day. George decided to try attaching a radio collar to a nomadic lion's neck and tracking it with a radio receiver.

By the 1960s, radio tracking had been used successfully on American bears, but never on an African predator. In the years to come, high-tech

George uses a receiver to pick up the signal from a lion's radio collar.

tags (using radio, acoustic, or satellite technology) would transform wildlife studies, allowing scientists to follow the travels of animals ranging from crickets to blue whales. But when George worked in the Serengeti, radio tracking was still a pioneering technology.

George chose a nomadic male with ear tag number 57 to become the first radio-tagged lion. He was a young fellow about three years old. George darted Lion 57 and, as the drugged beast slept, placed a radio collar around his scruffy neck. For four days and nights George and two assistants monitored the lion's every move by carrying a radio receiver in the Land Rover. When the signals from Lion 57's collar were strong, they knew he was nearby.

Lion 57 wandered for several days, scavenging hyena kills and occasionally resting peacefully with other nomadic lions. One evening 57 met another young lion at a waterhole. There was nothing to mark this event as special, yet from that moment the two males were inseparable.

George hoped to track Lion 57 for many months, but to his consternation the radio collar stopped working after a few days. He darted 57 again and removed his collar. Over the next two years George occasionally spotted Lion 57 and his companion on the plains and woodlands. They were beautiful, healthy animals. George hoped the pair would soon abandon their nomadic life, join a pride, and father many cubs.

Of all the Serengeti prides, George knew the Seronera pride and the Masai pride the best. He spent hours watching them. During the daytime lions were the couch potatoes of the Serengeti. An afternoon would drag by with no more action than a lazy flick of a black-tipped tail. Yet when the sun dropped, everything changed.

George loved watching lions on moonlit nights. He could observe without headlights or spotlights, which might alter the behavior of both the lions and their potential prey. Best of all, the Serengeti was magical in the silvery moonlight under an infinity of stars. Distant hyenas whooped, and the wind carried the crisp scent of hoof-crumpled grass. Wildness filled the air.

One night the Masai pride rose at dusk, yawned, stretched, and nuzzled one another. It was like a team warm-up and pep talk. The pride's ten cubs remained behind as its six lionesses trotted off, trailed by its two adult males, Black Mane and Brown Mane, who were trailed by George. Brown Mane was the most magnificent lion in the Serengeti. The great beast boasted such an extravagant ruff that George thought he looked like a wandering haystack.

The lionesses paused on a ridge to scan the valley below. As the shadows deepened, they split up and slipped away. The hunt was on.

Before long, George heard hoofbeats and a desperate, strangled scream. He sped along without headlights under the pale moon, trying to keep Black Mane and Brown Mane in sight, hoping the Land Rover wouldn't drop into a hidden ravine. Out of the darkness rose the terrifying snarls and savage growls of angry lionesses fighting for meat. The scent of blood drenched the air. Even though he was safe in the Land Rover, George shivered.

After gorging themselves, two of the lionesses left, returning an hour later with the pride's cubs in tow. By then Brown Mane had claimed the head, neck, and rib cage of the victim—a zebra. He shared his prize with the hungry cubs.

For several years the Seronera and Masai prides were fairly stable; each pride consisted of a pair of adult male lions, six adult females, and their cubs. Then one night the Seronera and Masai male lions went to war. The results were catastrophic.

The morning after the battle, George was shocked to find Yellow Mane of the Seronera pride lying mortally wounded. Bloody gashes crisscrossed his body, and chunks of mane littered the grass. He was like a rag doll with the stuffing ripped out.

Black Mane of the rival Masai pride emerged from the bushes to gaze at his dying rival. Yellow Mane gave one last growl, defiant to the end. Black Mane left. A few hours later, Yellow Mane's breaths slowly ebbed away and the fire faded from his eyes.

Yellow Mane's death set off a chain reaction. The remaining Seronera male fled, leaving the Seronera pride without any adult males. Its cubs were vulnerable. George had observed that when

Yellow Mane lies mortally wounded after his last battle.

new males take over a pride, they sometimes kill the cubs so that the pride lionesses will be able to mate as soon as possible. In this way the new males increase their chances of fathering cubs before being evicted by stronger rivals.

Eventually the Masai males, Black Mane and Brown Mane, left the Masai pride to join the Seronera lionesses. A pair of nomadic males took over the Masai pride. During these two years of turmoil, the Seronera and Masai lionesses lost two-thirds of their cubs. From their tragedy George learned that lionesses need a stable pride in order to raise young successfully.

This discovery had important implications for wildlife management. For many years hunters had argued that they should be allowed to shoot the "extra" male lions in a pride, since only one male was needed to father cubs. But George's research showed that killing males disrupts the pride's social structure and is disastrous for lions, lionesses, and cubs alike.

An irritated lioness snarls at a playful cub.

Even in the best of times, life was rough for lion cubs. Some were abandoned by their mothers; others were eaten by hyenas and leopards. Many starved to death. George learned that lions seesaw between generosity and utter selfishness. Male lions allow cubs to eat with them, yet they also crush strange cubs in their massive jaws. Lionesses will nurse any cub in the pride, but they often refuse to share a kill with their own starving young.

Watching cubs die of hunger was agonizing. As a scientist, George knew he was supposed to observe nature, not change its course. Yet he did this work because the animals delighted him, and he cared deeply about each one: the gorilla Mrs. Wrinkle and her baby, the tigress Cut-Ear and her cubs, and the littlest lions of the Serengeti.

One day George saw an old Seronera lioness carry her dying cub to the remains of a wildebeest. The three-week-old cub was pitifully skinny, covered in mud, and too weak even to lick a bone. George noticed that the mother's teats weren't swollen; she didn't have any milk. The lioness trotted away. Then, as George watched, a male lion picked the cub up in his jaws and dropped the little body. Vultures gathered expectantly.

This is what happens in the wild, George said to himself. *It's tragic, but I can't intervene . . .*

He drove home. "Look what I have in the car," George called.

Kay, Eric, and Mark were thrilled by the thin, dirty cub. They cleaned him up and laid him in a box with blankets and hot water bottles. By evening Kay had coaxed the cub into drinking a little milk. The next day he wobbled across their kitchen floor.

George named the cub Ramses, after an Egyptian pharaoh who went into battle with a lion by his side. From the first day Ramses was completely devoted to the Schaller pride. Yet he was still a lion. Ramses growled over his bottle as if it were a carcass to be defended, sometimes ripping off the nipple in a fury of possessiveness. He wrestled with the boys and stalked Kay around the house, leaping out unexpectedly from behind the sofa to grab her ankles. George felt like a lion himself when Ramses rubbed his cheek lovingly against George's, the lion equivalent of a hug.

George and Kay knew they couldn't keep Ramses. Lions are not meant to be pets; yet they could not put him back in the wild, because lions learn how to survive by being with other wild lions. Ramses left when he was four

Ramses plays with Mark.

months old and ultimately found a home at the Milwaukee Zoo, where he lived for many years and fathered many cubs. But the Schallers never forgot their little lion.

George's three-year immersion in lion country revealed much about the animals of the Serengeti. The ecosystem supported vast numbers of hoofed animals because each species exploited a different niche, just like the prey animals in India. Thomson's gazelles ate the tender shoots of grasses, wildebeests ate the leaves, and zebras ate the stems. Warthogs rooted for tubers, Cape buffalo ate coarse grasses, and giraffes nibbled treetops.

By carefully analyzing 1,803 kills, George found that each predator also had a specialty. Cheetahs took the slowest gazelles: the young, sick, or old. Leopards ate smaller antelopes, often lone males wandering too far from the herd. Wild dogs preferred young wildebeest and gazelles. Both hyenas and lions hunted adult wildebeest and zebra, but only lions could bring down adult Cape buffalo.

The predators' hunting methods also varied. A hoofed animal on the Serengeti was vulnerable to a short chase by a cheetah, a long chase by wild dogs or hyenas (wild dogs hunting mostly during the day, hyenas at night), or a sudden ambush by lions or leopards (lions in the plains or woodlands, leopards more often in dense thickets).

The prey animals weren't defenseless. Gazelles increased their chances by using speed, zebras and wildebeest bunched in herds, and warthogs dived into burrows. The end result was an intricate evolutionary dance between predator and prey, a constant, complex process of fine-tuning. The cheetah and the gazelle made each other fast; the lion and the buffalo made each other strong.

Before George began his study, some people thought the Serengeti predators should be reduced so that the hoofed animals might flourish.

George was able to show that predators took only about 9 to 10 percent of the available prey each year, an amount that helped to keep the population of hoofed animals at a size the Serengeti ecosystem could support. Without predators, the excess zebras, wildebeest, gazelle, and other grass-eaters would probably die of disease or of starvation brought on by overgrazing. As George put it, "Predators are the best wildlife managers."

George discovered that predator populations, in turn, were kept in check by the amount of available prey, the high death rates of cubs and pups, and by young adults moving away to seek new territories. Yet the protection of the park ended at its unmarked borders. Animals like Lion 57 had no way of knowing that the Serengeti's endless horizon was a mirage.

George watched Lion 57 and his lion friend grow into lordly beasts with lush manes. The pair wandered across the plains, hunting for game or, preferably, a carcass they could liberate from hyenas. One November day the pair roamed just outside the park's borders. The lions had no reason to flee a Land Rover; they had seen George's often enough. Even a man on foot was not particularly alarming. They had never been harmed by humans.

A foreign hunter on safari spotted the lions and drove near. He may or may not have gotten out of his car. Lion 57 may have turned to look, or not. If he was resting, he probably didn't bother to get up off the grass.

A few weeks later George received a yellow envelope in the mail. There was a letter from a hunting outfitter telling when and where the trophy animal had been taken. George tried to be grateful that the man had troubled to write, but it was hard not to feel bitter.

George tipped the envelope upside down. Into his hand dropped a bloodstained silver tag: Number 57.

Chapter 5: Cat Among the Clouds

PAKISTAN AND NEPAL, THE HIMALAYAS, 1969–1975

The Wakhi people of northern Pakistan believe that mountain goddesses inhabit the pure, sacred realm of the high Himalayas. These goddesses, they say, sometimes take the form of snow leopards, creatures of ethereal beauty and supernatural elusiveness.

In 1969 only a handful of Westerners had ever seen one of these legendary cats. Yet even the remote Himalayas, home to the world's highest mountains, had been penetrated by farmers, hunters, and herders. Its little-known wildlife was largely unprotected and declining rapidly.

George Schaller, now thirty-six, began a wide-ranging survey of snow leopards and the rare species of wild sheep and goats they prey upon. Over a six-year period (1969 to 1975) he spent a total of three years in the field. Kay, Eric, and Mark lived in Lahore, Pakistan, where the boys attended an international school. For the first time, George often worked far away from his family.

It was a lonely quest but an important one. George loved getting to know individual animals, but he knew many species were in danger of becoming

A painting of a snow leopard in the Potala Palace, Lhasa, Tibet.

extinct before they could be studied in detail. He felt a moral obligation to focus more of his efforts on conservation. In the Himalayas, George was on a mission—to find places that still sheltered healthy populations of wildlife and convince the governments of Nepal and Pakistan to turn the areas into national parks. If he failed, the snow leopard might vanish into myth and memory.

• • •

GEORGE SQUINTED AT THE MARKS IN THE SNOW. Not long ago a snow leopard had padded along this ridge. Here it had stopped to leave long scratch-marks, clawing down to bare dirt; there it had urinated; farther along, a pungent scent-mark lingered in the air. It was snow leopard graffiti.

These marks, found after weeks of searching, were the first evidence George had seen of snow leopards in Chitral Gol. This remote Pakistani valley was the private hunting ground of a former local ruler and home to Kashmir markhor, a species of wild goat that was a favorite prey of snow leopards. During winter the markhor moved from the high mountains into sheltered valleys, where they could be observed more easily. George had hoped he would also catch a glimpse of a snow leopard, but so far the cats had evaded him.

Paw prints left by the elusive snow leopard.

He bought five domestic goats, tethered them at different spots along the snow leopard's path, and fed and watered the goats daily. George had mixed feelings about using live goats to attract a snow leopard. He didn't want to see any animal suffer. Yet if he used dead goats, the bait would be quickly consumed by vultures and even more goats would be needed to attract a leopard. And his sympathies were with the endangered markhor, not domestic goats already destined for the stew pot. Every goat eaten by a snow leopard, George figured, spared a markhor.

Like the snow leopard, the markhor were rare and precious. Trophy hunters killed them for their tall, twisted horns while villagers shot them for meat. Now, in early December, it was markhor breeding season. The dominant male strutted around the females, head held high and chest ruff fluffing in the breeze. Sometimes a prancing male carefully sprayed urine on his own head and chest—a goatish version of cologne.

George sketched the markhor in his field notes.

A Kashmir markhor stands on the steep hillsides in Chitral Gol, part of the Hindu Kush mountains of Pakistan. *Hindu Kush* means "Hindu killer" because travelers, most of them Hindus, had such a difficult time crossing the mountains.

As the days passed, George saw many markhor but no leopards. One afternoon George's local guide ran up to him. The guide pointed excitedly toward a distant ridge where George had tethered a goat. Bearded vultures spiraled in the sky.

George pulled out his spotting scope. Had a leopard made a kill?

At first he saw only a patchwork of stone and snow. But there—on the crest of a cliff—lay a snow leopard, a female. She had small rounded ears, a white chin and chest, and paws so big they looked like oversized mittens.

Her coat was a beautiful blend of smoky gray and creamy white. She was almost invisible amid the snow-frosted rocks. To George's delight, near her was a small puffball: a four-month-old cub. It sat up, stretched, and lay down near its mother.

How close could he get? George walked slowly up the slope until he was several hundred feet from the ridge. The cub disappeared into the rocks. Its mother crouched low, silent and still as a sphinx, as she watched George.

George stayed near the mother and cub as the pale winter light faded into dusk and mist veiled the ridge. Snow fell. The land was soft, muted, peaceful.

At last the sky cleared. The rising moon painted the Himalayas in layers of silver light against a canvas of stars. It was ghostly quiet and utterly lovely, a landscape to match a leopard.

But the cats had vanished. George angled uphill, close to the spot where he had last seen them. His boots sank deep into the fresh snow.

56

Then he spotted the mother leopard lounging on a rock spur just fifty yards away. She sat up, her powder-blue eyes locked on George's. Neither moved.

The sky clouded over once more; mists swirled and snow drifted down. Snowflakes crowned the snow leopard's head and capped her shoulders. Embraced in her silent white world, George felt suspended somewhere between human and animal, reality and dream. Then the snow leopard disappeared, fading away like a tendril of smoke.

In the middle of the night, George retreated to his mountain hut, tired and frozen yet elated. When the sun rose, he hiked back to the slope. The mother and cub were still near the dead goat; the cub played among the rocks and chewed the carcass. After breakfast the little leopard bounced to its mother and rubbed its fluffy cheek lovingly against hers, just as the lion cub Ramses had once nuzzled George.

Every day George left out a new goat. The snow leopard usually attacked at night, but late one afternoon George witnessed a kill. She placed each paw silently and carefully as she stalked slowly downhill. When she reached a boulder above the goat, she leaped, landing just behind her prey. The goat whipped around to face her, horns lowered. She pulled back in surprise. But when the goat turned, the snow leopard seized it by the throat and kept her suffocating grip until the goat went limp.

The snow leopard in its element, among clouds and snow.

George watched the snow leopard and her cub for seven precious days. On the morning of the eighth day, all that remained were two sets of tracks disappearing into the mountains. There were no more snow leopards that season.

On a later visit to Chitral Gol, George received a message from Prince Burhan-ud-Din, a man who owned a private markhor reserve in nearby Tushi. Burhan-ud-Din knew of George's interest in leopards, and one had just been seen on his land.

"Where have you been?" Burhan-ud-Din asked when George arrived two days later. "My keeper shot the snow leopard yesterday. It was killing my markhor."

George was appalled. Snow leopards were officially protected in Pakistan, but apparently the law carried little weight. He looked sadly at the fresh skin hanging in a shed.

He doubted there were any more leopards around Tushi, but he left out a goat as bait, just in case. Two days later, to George's surprise, a snow leopard—a female—killed the goat and stayed by the carcass all day. Then as George watched in awe, she glided away until she seemed to fade into the rocks.

George learned that six snow leopards had been shot in the Chitral Gol area that year. When natural prey was scarce—usually because of overhunting or overgrazing by livestock—the leopards killed domestic animals. Villagers then killed the snow leopards to protect their flocks.

Snow leopards had other refuges besides Chitral Gol, however. George heard about a place called Shey, a Buddhist monastery in northern Nepal near the Tibetan border, where by local tradition no hunting was allowed. The bharal (also called blue sheep) around Shey were said to be plentiful and tame. Bharal were very odd creatures; scientists couldn't decide whether they were goats or sheep. The species had never been studied in the wild, so George decided to travel to Shey in late autumn in hopes of observing the bharal mating season. And if there were bharal at Shey, there might also be snow leopards.

The expedition to Shey included writer Peter Matthiessen (a friend of George's), fifteen porters, and four Sherpas (a Himalayan people famous for their ability to live and work at high altitudes). Everyone carried heavy packs of food and equipment. There were no roads to Shey and no airstrips. The monastery lay on the other side of the Himalayas, which Swedish explorer Sven Hedin called "the gigantic wall which Nature has built up like a bulwark to guard the secrets of Tibet."

They left Pokhara, Nepal, in late September. Their route took them west along the lower slopes of two great mountains, Annapurna and Dhaulagiri, both over 26,000 feet high. When the skies cleared, they could see the ice-bright summits looming impossibly high on the horizon. Past the peaks they turned north.

Along the way George shared his knowledge of Himalayan plants and animals with Peter. In turn, Peter taught George about Buddhism, a religion practiced by many Himalayan peoples.

George was anxious to climb higher. "I wish we were up at 8,000 feet right now," he told Peter. "I like crisp air." Peter found George's hiking ability formidable. "[If it] were not for the slow pace of the porters," Peter wrote, "he would run me into the ground."

The trip was often frustrating. George, Peter, and the Sherpas huddled for days in sodden villages when rain turned the footpath into a muddy cascade. Blood-hungry leeches clung to their ankles. They ate mostly oatmeal, rice, and boiled potatoes. It was difficult to keep porters because nobody wanted to cross the mountains in late autumn.

Often the trail seemed better suited for mountain goats than pack-laden humans. Near Phoksumdo Lake the route narrowed into a thin ledge running along a cliff. At one frightening spot there was no ledge at all, just flat stones jutting haphazardly from the rock face. Between the gaps—a hundred feet down—turquoise lake waters sparkled.

Peter later wrote about crawling along, terrified, on his hands and knees. When he reached a wider ledge he stopped to let his pounding heart quiet. Stepping past him, sure-footed George remarked, "This is the first *really* interesting stretch of trail we've had so far."

For all the discomfort and difficulty, there were many enchanting moments. The mountains were pure and brilliant as diamonds, faceted with slivers of shining waterfalls. As they neared Shey, George spotted his favorite birds wheeling overhead: a playful pair of ravens. It seemed a good omen.

Peter Matthiessen (in blue coat) with Sherpas Tukten (left), Jung-bu, Gyaltsen, and Dawa at the summit of a 16,900-foot pass with the Tibetan highlands stretching northward.

The final pass stood 17,600 feet high, ringed by a garland of mountains. As they descended, they saw the square walls of Shey Monastery against a brindled backdrop of earth and snow. A band of blue-gray bharal grazed nearby on the treeless hillside. Above it all loomed Crystal Mountain.

According to legend, Crystal Mountain was once home to an evil god. A Buddhist monk defeated the god with the help of a flying snow leopard. That day there were no snow leopards to be seen, flying or otherwise. Yet

Shey Monastery at the foot of Crystal Mountain.

Young bharal clamber among the rocks.

after a five-week, 250-mile trek, Shey was a welcome sight. George's study of bharal—and perhaps snow leopards—could finally begin.

THE BHARAL MATING SEASON started with a resounding *CRACK!* Thuds echoed across Shey's hillsides as pairs of males reared up and crashed down with ferocious force on each other's horns. Yet the male bharal didn't always fight. When feeling submissive, a male stroked his head against another male's butt. Sometimes George saw several bharal in a rump-rubbing conga line.

George noticed that male bharal fought like goats, yet rubbing was a typical sheep behavior (though sheep rubbed faces, not rumps). From these and many other behavioral clues, George decided bharal were slightly more goatlike than sheeplike. The common ancestor of sheep and goats, George concluded, probably resembled a bharal.

George counted several hundred bharal around Shey, yet few young. He

60

suspected poor habitat was to blame rather than predation from wolves or leopards. Only a few people lived at Shey during the winter, but villagers brought livestock to graze in the spring and summer. Hungry mouths and sharp hooves destroyed the meager plant life, leaving nothing to hold the depleted topsoil. Shey was a wounded land.

After two weeks at Shey, George and Peter found the first sign of a snow leopard: a paw print in the dirt. They followed the tracks and discovered scratch marks here and there. On a rock outcrop lay a fresh mound of feces. "Isn't that something," George said, smiling, "to be so delighted with a pile of crap?" He tucked it into a plastic bag.

They scanned the rocks with binoculars. A golden eagle swept along the cliffs, borne on winds from the top of the world, but they could not spot the snow leopard. George suspected that it was watching them, unseen, from some stony perch.

The next day, and the next, they found fresh snow leopard tracks and scratch marks. George set up a camera trap (a camera-and-tripwire combination set up to photograph whatever crosses its path). The snow leopard walked around it. After four days there were no more signs of the mystery leopard; it had moved on. The small size of the bharal herd at Shey—only about two hundred animals—indicated to George that Shey lacked sufficient prey to support a resident snow leopard.

After a month at Shey George's supplies were low. Peter had left earlier to return to his family. Now it was time for George to go, too. He had promised to join Kay and the boys in Pakistan for Christmas. If he did not leave soon, heavy snow might trap him at Shey until spring.

George went out for a last walk in the shadow of Crystal Mountain. This was his purest pleasure, to wander in the wild without aim or expectation. As he squinted at a set of tracks made by a vole (a small rodent), some instinct made him glance upward. The head of a great white wolf peeked over the hilltop like a rising moon. The wolf gazed serenely at George. *Such a creature,* George thought, awed. *Power and beauty, inseparable.*

Two blond wolves joined the white one. Suddenly, as if drawn by an invisible thread, all three disappeared. George climbed to the crest of the bare hill, but nothing moved except wispy clouds. The wolves had vanished like wraiths.

In all his Himalayan wanderings George spotted only a few snow leopards. He found just 29 sets of tracks and gathered just 47 feces. Yet this scant information was more than anyone else had ever collected. George knew that snow leopards were mostly solitary (25 out of 29 tracks were made by lone cats). He did not have enough data to calculate the size of a leopard's home range, but he knew from the scarcity of their prey that the cats must roam large areas.

The snow leopard feces he analyzed revealed that Chitral Gol's cats ate as much livestock as they did markhor, while those around Shey ate mostly bharal and marmots (a large rodent). The leopards—especially those in Chitral Gol—needed healthy populations of natural prey to keep them alive and away from livestock, much like the tigers he had studied in India.

This yak caravan helped George and his Sherpa companions find their way over a high pass during a snowstorm.

George knew Chitral Gol, Shey, and other areas of the Himalayas were promising areas for national parks. Protection of these places by the governments of Pakistan and Nepal was desperately needed, not just for snow leopards but for the entire community of Himalayan life, from head-bashing bharal to delicate wildflowers. To save these wild lands George needed to be a diplomat as well as a scientist and conservationist.

On the morning George left Shey, one of the Sherpas tossed incense into the coals of their final fire, an offering to bring good luck on their journey. They had been warned to take a different route back, because some passes were already closed by snow. Their new path was still difficult. A blizzard hit just as they climbed toward the last high pass. They stumbled blindly inside the snowy whirlwind, unable to find the route up. Then the sweet sound of bells trickled down the mountain and a yak caravan approached out of the whiteness. The men and animals plodded by and vanished, but at last George and his companions had trail markers—frozen droppings left behind by the yaks. At the summit they found tattered prayer flags tied to a wooden pole, offerings thanking the mountain gods for safe passage. George silently added his own heartfelt gratitude.

Their route took them through more deep snow and across icy rivers. When George's group entered a narrow, sunless gorge, the footpath turned into a snow-covered ledge across an outward-sloping cliff. They had to shuffle sideways along the ledge, clinging to tiny fingerholds as their heels hung over the chasm.

At last they emerged from the dark, frozen gorge and stepped into a sunlit valley. The snow glittered. George knew this was his last day in the wilds of Nepal; they would soon descend into valleys lined with villages. He still hadn't seen a snow leopard on the trip, but after all the hard days of trekking to Shey and back, George was so tired he was hardly able to feel the disappointment.

Something made him glance toward a small meadow patched with snow. There before him—was it real?—stood a snow leopard!

Warm pleasure filled George. Then the ghostly gray cat bounded away with effortless leaps, sailing across a stream, through a thicket, and into a jumble of rocks. With a last flick of its plush tail, the snow leopard melted into the mountains.

(map) Beijing ★ · CHINA · TIBETAN PLATEAU · WOLONG NATURE RESERVE · Chengdu · Shanghai · Hong Kong · o Miles 500 · o Kilometers 1000

Chapter 6: Panda Politics

CENTRAL CHINA, 1980–1985

The endearing panda, most strikingly colored of all mammals, evolved along the eastern edge of the Tibetan Plateau. Like Africa's mountain gorillas, China's pandas were stranded in small patches of mountainous terrain as their forests were cut down and turned into farmland. Yet even among snow-bound heights, pandas were not safe. Villagers shot and snared them for their pelts and trapped them for zoos.

A Chinese government survey conducted in 1974-1977 found only about 1,000 pandas left in the wild. In 1980 China agreed to collaborate with the World Wildlife Fund on research to help save the panda. The project needed a well-respected scientist, someone who had done pioneering fieldwork on rare mammals, a dedicated conservationist able to keep going in the face of hardship. In short, the project needed George Schaller.

For George, now forty-seven, China's pandas presented a strange new conservation problem: they were in danger of being loved to death.

• • •

A panda eating bamboo. Bamboo is a low-quality food, so pandas can't build up stores of fat. Unlike most other bears, pandas don't hibernate.

"DAXIONGMAO! PANDA!"

George and Kay peeked out of their tent to see a Chinese co-worker running toward them, arms flapping in excitement. They all dashed up the trail. Winter's snow was turning slushy underfoot and wet bamboo leaves sent little cold showers down their necks, but nothing could dampen their enthusiasm.

Ahead they spotted the box trap, baited with goat meat. (Although pandas have evolved to live on bamboo, they will eat meat and are attracted to its smell.) The panda inside almost filled the trap. It gave a pitiful hoot of distress, chomped its teeth together, and let out a forest-shaking roar. Everyone, including George, instinctively jumped back. A moment later they were all laughing nervously.

But the daylight was fading fast. George decided they should radio-collar the panda in the morning. Kay and the rest of the team went back to camp for the night while George and Howard Quigley, an American bear expert, slept in the forest to keep an eye on the panda.

It was a restless night for George, and not just because of the cold and lumpy ground. Basic research on wild pandas was needed to develop a conservation plan for the species. Yet pandas were extremely difficult to find and follow; their rugged mountain home combined the dense foliage of the gorilla forest with the high altitude and freezing cold of the snow leopard's realm. Radio-collaring would allow the researchers to track pandas even when the animals couldn't be observed directly. It would provide data on their movements and on their interactions with other radio-collared pandas. George hoped to answer important questions: How much space does a panda require to satisfy its need for food and mates? What happens when pandas cross paths?

Yet from his experience with lions, George knew that sedating and radio-collaring an animal involved risk. Pandas were Chinese national treasures. The death of a single panda would haunt George forever and might cause the Chinese government to shut down the entire project.

He listened anxiously to the panda chewing on the logs of her cage. *What if she chokes on the wood?* George shined his flashlight into the cage and caught the eerie glow of her eyes. She was fine.

The next morning Kay and the rest of the research team, including Hu

Jinchu and Pan Wenshi, returned. George was accustomed to working alone in the field, but on this project he was training and collaborating with Chinese scientists. Professor Hu Jinchu was a gentle man who enjoyed fieldwork and had already spent several years conducting a wildlife survey. George and Hu Jinchu were co-directors of the panda project. Pan Wenshi was a laboratory scientist with no previous field experience but plenty of energy and enthusiasm.

Howard Quigley stuck the caged panda in the thigh with a pole mounted syringe. Nothing happened; the panda's tough hide had bent the needle. He tried again. "Okay, got her!"

The panda gradually slumped down. They pulled her out of the cage to examine her. She had blunt yellow teeth, a sign of middle age. Hu Jinchu checked her nipples. No milk, which meant no cub. Pan Wenshi looked for fleas and ticks but found nothing. George cradled her black forepaw and gazed curiously at one of the wonders of evolution: the panda's "thumb." Their special sixth digit (actually a modified wrist bone) enables pandas to pluck and eat bamboo with great dexterity.

It took everyone to weigh her: 190 pounds. Then George and Howard fixed the radio collar around the sleeping panda's neck.

"Don't forget to take off the magnet," Kay reminded them. Removing the magnet would turn on the radio collar.

While Zhen-Zhen is sedated, Pan Wenshi and Hu Jinchu check her nipples for signs that she is nursing an infant. The team later put a radio collar on Zhen-Zhen.

Once the collar was activated, they pulled the panda back into the trap so that she wouldn't hurt herself while half-awake. An hour later she was alert and cranky. They raised the door, but the panda merely sat timidly in the cage. Finally, after a quick peek, she rushed out. All they could see was swaying bamboo as she crashed away into the forest.

The Chinese named her Zhen-Zhen ("precious"). Zhen-Zhen was a very practical panda. Having learned that cages offered free meals, she traveled from trap to trap, gobbled the bait, and waited grumpily until someone appeared to release Her Preciousness.

Wolong's dramatic landscape made it a difficult place to track wild pandas.

Despite Zhen-Zhen's best efforts to occupy all the traps, George and his team successfully captured and radio-collared five other pandas. Long-Long ("dragon"), a shy young male, was named after their study site, Wolong Nature Reserve. *Wolong* means "resting dragon." When fog gathered along the ridges, the mountain did resemble a slumbering dragon encased in its own smoky breath.

Ning-Ning ("gentle") was a young female who behaved like a pet. She leaned against the bars of the cage to be scratched, ate from the scientists' hands, and let them hold and stroke her forepaw. Because Ning-Ning and Zhen-Zhen often spent time in the same part of the forest, George suspected Ning-Ning was Zhen-Zhen's daughter.

Wei-Wei ("grand"), an older male, covered his face with his paws as he sat in the trap. He seemed to be trying to hide, or praying that this would all be over soon. Han-Han ("lovely but inept") was so perfect a panda she looked as if she'd just arrived from a toy factory. Pi-Pi ("brave") proved to be the dominant male in the Wolong study area. Massive Pi-Pi roared a few times, but for the most part he endured his temporary captivity with quiet dignity.

By tracking the radio-collared pandas, George and his team learned that pandas have small home ranges (about two square miles). Although pandas aren't social, their ranges often overlap. Pandas mark their home areas with scent from a gland under their tail. Certain trees were bulletin boards, their trunks stained with hundreds of pungent panda messages.

That fall Zhen-Zhen's radio signal showed she was spending most of her time around a den site—a hollow in the base of a massive fir tree. In

October, George and Hu Jinchu went to check on her. Zhen-Zhen emerged, roaring and snorting. A loud squawk came from the den. A cub! George and Hu Jinchu slipped quietly away.

Four days later Zhen-Zhen's radio signal showed she had left the den area. George found a huge pile of panda feces at the den entrance. The nest itself was spotless, nicely cushioned by a pile of wood chips Zhen-Zhen had clawed from the walls. For some reason she had also dragged in a five-foot-tall fir tree. Was it camouflage? Or whimsy?

They looked forward to watching Zhen-Zhen with a roly-poly cub, but it was not to be. When they saw her again, she was alone. Had a marten (a kind of large weasel), a leopard, or a golden cat (a small wild feline) killed the infant? Or had Zhen-Zhen lost it? They would never know.

Pandas spent almost all their time eating, and George, Kay, and the rest of the team spent almost all their time gathering data on what the pandas ate. The radio collars allowed the researchers to trail along after the pandas and gather the feces, greenish lumps that smelled like fresh-cut grass. The feces were taken to camp and dried. The remains of leaves, stems, and shoots were carefully separated and counted. Sometimes so many drying panda droppings lay around the Schallers' small tent that the place reminded George of a stable.

The work was tedious but essential to understanding pandas. By measuring how much bamboo pandas eat compared to the amount of bamboo in the forest, they could roughly calculate how many pandas an area of habitat could support.

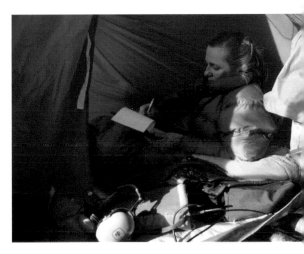

Kay records the position of the radio-collared pandas. From this tent pitched high on a ridge, the research team was able to pick up the signals from several pandas at once.

Zhen-Zhen usually stayed high on Wolong's slopes eating the leaves and stems of arrow bamboo shaded by towering fir trees. But each spring she ventured down to feast on sprouts of umbrella bamboo, a species that grows at a slightly lower altitude. One day George glimpsed Zhen-Zhen as she used her paws and teeth to shuck bamboo shoots like ears of corn and then eat the tender cores. She fed herself with hardly a wasted motion. In the course of a day, the 190-pound panda could gobble 600 shoots weighing 66 pounds.

Samples of the bamboo species eaten by Zhen-Zhen and other pandas were sent to a lab for analysis. When combined with the field research, the results showed that pandas must stuff themselves to survive. Their simple digestive tract is designed for a traditional bear diet—meat, seeds, and fruit. Long ago, however, pandas switched to bamboo, a plentiful but low-quality food. To meet its nutritional needs on a bamboo diet, a panda must keep its stomach constantly full. The panda is like a car powered by a truck-load of woodchips instead of a gallon of gas.

Even when tracking a radio-collared panda, the scientists seldom actually saw one amid the thick maze of bamboo that covered Wolong's slopes. Pleasant weather was rare; when it wasn't snowing at Wolong, it was raining. The most common forest sound was *drip . . . drip . . . drip*. George often shivered in damp clothes, his fingers so frozen he could barely write notes. "The essence of panda tracking," George wrote, "is discomfort."

Yet the forest also offered small treasures: tiny tufted deer that looked like rodents on twiggy legs, orange-crested Tragopan pheasants, and beautiful golden monkeys. Sometimes over a hundred monkeys rushed through the treetops above George, screaming like excited children.

George occasionally saw leopard droppings and paw prints in the forest. The droppings usually contained the hair of musk deer, tufted deer, or golden monkeys. One day Pan Wenshi was walking down a trail when he came across a leopard basking in a patch of sunlight. Afterward, he told George: "I am much afraid!"

Yet the most dangerous animal in Wolong, as in most places, was man. That fall George found wire snares set by musk deer poachers. It was bad enough to kill rare musk deer, but the pandas could also be caught in the snares. Woodcutters had plundered the forest, too. Raw stumps littered one slope. When George complained, his Chinese co-workers said that nothing could be done.

China was just emerging from the chaos and violence of the Cultural Revolution. The government had jailed or even killed many people, especially educated Chinese. Only now was China opening up and allowing foreign scientists like George into the country. Most Chinese, however, were still afraid of their government. They were reluctant to speak out, even when something illegal was going on. This was deeply frustrating for George.

Kay's presence was a great comfort. Now that Eric and Mark were in college, she was able to join George in the field again. They talked about happy times in Africa and India. And they reminded each other how lucky they were to be able to express their opinions, come and go as they pleased, and make their dreams a reality.

To raise everyone's spirits during the dreary winter, George and Kay planned some Christmas cheer at Wolong. Their first task was a visit to Zhen-Zhen's abandoned den. The little fir tree was still there. Kay gently lifted it out. The tree was spindly and panda-chewed yet somehow perfect.

Kay was delighted. "A present from Zhen-Zhen to us!"

They carried the little fir back to the research camp. With its muddy trails, sagging canvas tents, and rotting garbage piles, the camp always reminded George of an old-time Gold Rush town. Yet on Christmas Day the soggy outpost was bright with fellowship. The cooks created a banquet, and one of their Chinese colleagues made a snow panda with coal-blackened eyes and ears. George and Hu Jinchu offered toasts to the project's success, and Kay led an off-key round of "Silent Night."

The highlight was Zhen-Zhen's Christmas tree. It filled the smoky communal hut with a sweet fir-tree scent. George and Kay added ornaments brought from home: paper-and-pipe-cleaner Santas and elves made by Eric and Mark in Africa; tin blackbuck, chital, and tigers George had cut from can lids to decorate their tree in India. Their Chinese colleagues contributed papier-mâché pandas and golden monkeys made of glass. It was an unusual Christmas, but one they would never forget.

The female panda strangled in a poacher's snare is carried out of the forest.

AFTER A PROMISING START, the panda project's next few years were plagued by a series of deaths. The radio collars on gentle Ning-Ning and lovely Han-Han stopped working. Neither panda was seen again. A poacher was later arrested for killing Han-Han in a snare meant for musk deer.

One day George was hiking through a part of Wolong where illegal woodcutters had been at work. Across scattered stumps he spotted the silvery white back of a reclining panda. He crouched down and waited. Nothing happened. Angling away to get a better view, George realized why the panda was so still.

The panda had walked into the noose of a snare tied to a small sapling. She might have crushed the sapling in her jaws, but instinct urged her to pull away. The panda had retreated around a clump of bamboo, circling again and again as the wire tightened around her neck and strangled her.

George knelt at the dead panda's side and stroked her back. He was overwhelmed by the suffering of this innocent creature and furious at the officials who might have prevented it, if only they had patrolled the forest and enforced antipoaching laws.

The next morning George, Hu Jinchu, and the Wolong park staff carried the panda's body down the mountain. The poacher was never caught.

There was more trouble that year: all the arrow bamboo flowered. Flowers are usually a sign of hope and renewal, but when a bamboo species mass-flowers, it dies.

Bamboo has a strange life cycle. Usually the plant reproduces from shoots that sprout every spring from underground stems. But at irregular intervals of 15 to 120 years, a bamboo species will flower all at once and then die off. Lush green forests become dead stubble. The bamboo eventually grows again, but it takes months or years for the forests to return to normal. During the previous bamboo die-off in 1975, several hundred pandas had starved. Could the remaining pandas survive this new catastrophe?

Newspapers all around the world carried stories about helpless, starving pandas. Aid poured in. Half a million Chinese children donated money to help the pandas, and American children began a "Pennies for Pandas" campaign. The Chinese government used the money to launch a panda rescue effort. They bought trucks and built rescue centers. Rewards were offered to anyone bringing in a starving panda.

George knew that pandas were totally dependent on bamboo. Yet the species had been around long enough to survive plenty of bamboo die-offs. The Wolong research team watched their study animals carefully and found that as the arrow bamboo flowered and died, the Wolong pandas

simply moved down to lower elevations to feed on a different species, the umbrella bamboo.

George surveyed other panda reserves, too. In a few places only the dying arrow bamboo was available because panda habitat at lower elevations had been turned into farmland. Those pandas did need special help. Most pandas, however, were able to move around and find enough bamboo to eat.

Most endangered species don't get much attention. Little or no money is spent to save them, either by governments or individuals. The panda was perhaps the most adorable animal on the planet. People cared. But was the "Save the Panda" campaign really saving any pandas?

George felt that most panda conservation money should be used to enlarge panda reserves and create antipoaching patrols. If that were done, wild pandas would be safe and have a variety of bamboo in time of need. Only a few pandas needed to be rescued; most were far better off in the wild. But soon, even keeping Zhen-Zhen wild became a problem.

George and Kay left Wolong for a few months to spend time with Eric and Mark in the United States. When George returned, he was warned not to sleep in his tent: "A panda is using it." George found panda droppings on his bed and an impressive pile in a corner. In all the years he'd been collecting feces for analysis, this was the first time an animal had delivered it to him!

George moved to the bunkhouse. As he unpacked, Zhen-Zhen arrived in camp, growling and snorting. One of the Chinese workers threw her a hunk of sugarcane; as soon as she was finished, she was given another.

George learned that Zhen-Zhen had visited camp one day and a worker thought it would be amusing to feed her. Now she wouldn't leave. George realized that Zhen-Zhen was a cranky beggar because she had been trained to be one. He asked the staff to stop feeding her. Instead, Chinese officials decided to put Zhen-Zhen in captivity. George argued that they only needed to move her to a different part of Wolong and stop feeding her. No one listened.

Zhen-Zhen visits the communal hut at the Wolong research station in search of food.

George visited Zhen-Zhen a few months later at a center for captive pandas. She wandered listlessly around her concrete pen. She was fat and dull. *Left in the wild, she would have found a mate,* George thought. *Zhen-Zhen should be in Wolong with a newborn cub, not in a cage.*

George campaigned stubbornly to win Zhen-Zhen's release, while Hu Jinchu worked quietly to support George's efforts. Finally they were successful. After four months as a captive, Zhen-Zhen was released in Wolong about ten miles from her old home range. She visited camp once, but when no one fed her she moved on. She was a wild panda once again.

The four and a half years of the panda project was a difficult time for George. The Wolong research succeeded in providing much new information on pandas—how far they roam, how they interact with each other, and how they survive on an all-bamboo diet, both in normal times and during a bamboo die-off. At the same time, not much was done to save the remaining wild pandas.

Yet the panda project did help build conservation awareness throughout China. And the government did start protecting more panda habitat. Looking back, George says his memories of the pandas "have not faded, but they shuttle between heartache and happiness."

One of George's favorite memories was a forest encounter with Zhen-Zhen. He radio-tracked her to a dense patch of bamboo. In the green twilight George listened to her feed. *Snap. Crunch. Crunch. Snap.*

Zhen-Zhen back where she belongs: in the wild.

Zhen-Zhen rose and pushed her barrel-shaped body through the screen of bamboo. She gazed shyly at George. Her luminous round face reminded him of a full moon on a frosty night. She bobbed her head and snorted softly.

Satisfied that George was no threat, Zhen-Zhen sat back against a stand of bamboo. She bleated gently as a lamb and laid her forepaws serenely across her round white belly.

George was charmed. *She looks like a meditating Buddha,* he thought.

Her chin dropped. Her gentle bleats grew faint and stopped. Zhen-Zhen had fallen asleep.

Zhen-Zhen still inhabits George's thoughts. She pushes gently through the bamboo and lifts her eyes to his. Then she retreats inside herself, to a place without cages or collars. Just a green infinity of bamboo, the panda's Eden. No human can follow her there. Not even George.

Chapter 7: Asses and Antelopes

THE TIBETAN PLATEAU, WESTERN CHINA, 1985–PRESENT

As a boy, George Schaller was thrilled by Swedish explorer Sven Hedin's books about the Chang Tang, high on the Tibetan Plateau. "All distances and dimensions are cast on such a gigantic scale," wrote Hedin, "that you may march for weeks at a time and still find the situation unchanged—still find yourself the centre of a universe of mountains."

George never lost his longing for this special place. "Is it possible to be homesick for a world unknown?" he wrote.

In 1985, fifty-two-year-old George finally visited the Chang Tang. Tibetan antelopes, wild yaks, gazelles, wild asses, wolves, bears, and lynxes roamed its rolling hills and broad plains. Its people were hardy Tibetans who rode shaggy ponies and lived in yak-hair tents. The Chang Tang was still China's wild, wild West.

Not since the Murie expedition in Alaska had George seen such a wilderness. He hoped to make the Chang Tang the Chinese equivalent of America's Arctic National Wildlife Refuge: an entire ecosystem protected in its natural state.

Kiang (Tibetan wild asses) range across the Chang Tang.

Yet even the remote Chang Tang was threatened. To save it, George would need to unravel a mystery involving New York society ladies, Indian smugglers, Tibetan nomads, and the fatal beauty of the world's finest wool.

• • •

IT WAS EASY TO FEEL TINY AS A GNAT on the stark plains of the Chang Tang. Yet George felt at home in this barren place, where not even a shrub stood against the scouring wind. He left camp behind and hiked up and over a ridge. A black boulder huddled at the top of the ridge, odd and conspicuous in the gray-brown landscape. As George approached, the "boulder" suddenly rose from the earth.

The wild yak was a ton of muscle with great curving horns and shaggy fur falling almost to its feet, a prehistoric cave painting come to life. Bold and alert, it stared at George. George understood how our ancestors must have felt in the presence of such a creature: very, very small. He backed slowly away.

George had come to the Chang Tang to survey its wildlife, and he hoped his data would inspire the Chinese government to protect this vast high-altitude (15,000 to 17,000 feet) rangeland. George visited almost every year, driving hundreds of miles through high passes, along valleys, and across plains and basins. He counted the number and kind of animals he saw in different areas and used the numbers from these samples to estimate how many wild animals the Chang Tang sheltered.

The wild yak bull stares at George in Tibet's Chang Tang Reserve. *Chang Tang* means "northern plain" in Tibetan.

Sometimes George would come across a herd of kiang (also called Tibetan wild asses), two-toned animals of chestnut brown and creamy white. The kiang would race alongside George's car, then veer away in a cloud of dust and whipping tails. Over eighty years earlier, explorer Sven Hedin had witnessed thousands of elegant kiang running and turning in perfect formation, as if guided by invisible riders.

Delicate Tibetan gazelles also lived in the Chang Tang. One day George noticed a female near camp. She bounded frantically in the air as if to say, *Look at me!* George suspected she was drawing attention to herself for a reason. He found it nearby—a fawn flattened against the ground, absolutely still, innocent eyes open wide. George retreated quietly so that mother and baby could reunite.

Near the gazelles George counted over two hundred wild yaks, a big herd by today's standards. In Sven Hedin's time yak herds were so vast they blackened the hills, but decades of overhunting for meat and hides had taken a heavy toll. Now wild yak survived only in the most remote parts of the Chang Tang.

A group of yaks suddenly bolted; with their massive square forms they resembled galloping sofas. Five wolves zigzagged among the yaks. George guessed that the predators were searching for a vulnerable calf, but there were no young ones in the herd. The yaks finally halted and wheeled around to face the milling wolves. Defeated by the imposing wall of horn and hide, the wolves trotted away.

Other Chang Tang predators included shaggy Tibetan bears and plush lynxes. On one trip, Kay and a Tibetan driver were traveling across a plain when a female bear with two cubs emerged from a hollow. The mother bear charged their vehicle, teeth bared, every hair bristling. The driver hastily accelerated and they escaped the bear's wrath. When she returned to camp, Kay told George, "I have never, ever seen such an angry animal."

One day George spotted two fledgling saker falcons perched on a rocky pinnacle. As he watched the young birds, he noticed another cliff dweller nearby: a sandy-haired lynx. The lynx looked at George with such relaxed innocence that he suspected it had never seen a human before. That was not surprising. The area was so barren that local hawks added the scavenged horns of chiru (also known as the Tibetan antelope) to their nests because they couldn't find enough sticks. George guessed that the lynx survived in the desolate land by preying upon Tibetan wooly hares.

The chiru was the most common hoofed animal in the Chang Tang. Chiru looked so much like African antelope that the Chang Tang sometimes reminded George of a snowy Serengeti. Yet chiru weren't antelope at all; they belonged to the sheep and goat family. The chiru's ancestors may have descended from the mountains to live in the grasslands and then evolved to resemble other plains-dwelling animals. Sven Hedin had written: "It is hard to imagine a more beautiful spectacle than these agile, elegant animals presented, with their shiny horns sparkling like bayonets in the sunshine."

Two male chiru threaten each other while another watches.

Winter was chiru breeding season, when herds gathered along the northern edge of the grasslands. George traveled there by truck and car with a team of Tibetan and Han Chinese biologists to count the chiru and observe their mating behavior. The cold was brutal; temperatures could reach forty degrees below zero. In the mornings it was so frigid that their driver had to heat the engine with a blowtorch just to get the truck started. George sometimes felt as if his eyeballs were freezing.

Their hardships were rewarded when George found dozens of chiru assembled in a basin. The winter coats of the males were striking: black markings on their face and legs contrasted with their tawny bodies and snowy throats. They stood very tall and neatly spaced as small groups of female chiru "shopped" for a mate, wandering casually from male to male.

George walked slowly out among the chiru. He sat down and curled into his best imitation of a rock. At first the animals scattered, but soon they forgot George. He was just a lump on the landscape.

A female chiru sauntered up to a male. He lifted his chin, pranced, bellowed, and flashed his fluffy white tail, trying to look as impressive as possible. One female sprinted away with an eager male close behind. Two other males sparred—rather gingerly—with their sharp horns. A wolf passed like a shadow across a distant hilltop as twittering larks flowed by on a stream of wind. George felt immersed in the pure energy of the Chang Tang.

Basing his calculations on the size of their habitat and the writings of early explorers, who described herds numbering in the tens of thousands, George estimated that a million chiru once roamed the Tibetan Plateau. Yet he found relatively few during his wildlife surveys. The chiru he did see were shy and often ran at the first sight of a vehicle. George heard rumors of poachers organizing hunts in which hundreds of chiru, males and females alike, were slaughtered with high-powered rifles. The hunters skinned the carcasses and left the meat to rot. Orphaned fawns slowly starved to death.

One day George's team came across a poacher's camp. Frozen chiru carcasses were piled next to severed heads; the hides were neatly folded inside a tent. Clearly, the chiru hides were valuable. And when George visited villages, he sometimes saw traders plucking wool from chiru hides. Yet the nomads used the wool of domestic yaks, not chiru wool, to make their tents and clothing. Where was the chiru wool going? What was it used for?

When George asked the traders, they said they didn't know. They sold their chiru wool to other traders, who sold the wool yet again. George was alarmed and frustrated. Few people had ever heard of the Chang Tang or its chiru. Yet a great tragedy was unfolding in this little-known corner of the world.

A poacher at his hunting camp. Nomads can sell chiru hides for at least thirty dollars each, a lot of money in a place where many people live on a few hundred dollars a year.

George's survey team was camped near a village one day when a government official stopped by to say hello. George politely asked if the wildlife laws were being enforced. "Hunting has been banned. There is no hunting now," the official insisted. George couldn't help noticing the freshly shot Tibetan gazelle sprawled in the back of the official's Toyota.

To help the animals of the Chang Tang, George tried to appeal to the religious values of nomads like Chida, an elderly Tibetan who had lived in the Chang Tang all his life. Chida invited George and Kay into his yak-hair tent and served them salted tea mixed with yak butter. George gave Chida a gift, a special card he gave to all the nomads he met during his travels. The card showed a Buddhist saint surrounded by peaceful animals and a hunter who has given up his sword, bow, and arrows. On the opposite side was a Buddhist saying written in Tibetan:

> *All beings tremble at punishment,*
> *To all life is dear.*
> *Comparing others to oneself,*
> *One should neither kill nor cause to kill.*

Nomads of the Chang Tang.

Chida touched the card reverently to his forehead. Like most Tibetans, he was a devout Buddhist and did not believe in needless killing. But his family was poor. And officials drove into the Chang Tang from nearby towns to shoot chiru. Chida told George and Kay that if he didn't kill the animals, the outsiders would. "If the officials obey the law and stop hunting, we will, too," Chida promised.

One day George received a letter from Michael Sautman, a wool merchant in California who had heard George was an expert on Tibetan wildlife. The merchant was researching shahtoosh, a rare wool that was the softest and finest in the world. Supposedly, shahtoosh was the winter coat of the "Tibetan ibex" (the ibex is a wild mountain goat), which shed its wool naturally. Nomads, it was said, picked the wool from rocks and bushes. Traders bought the wool and sold it in India, where it was woven into expensive shawls. Was it true, Sautman asked, that the wool came from an ibex? And that the ibex was not killed?

George knew there was no such animal as a "Tibetan ibex." Shahtoosh must be chiru wool. Now he understood why the chiru were being slaughtered. But how could the trade in chiru wool be stopped?

George asked Sautman and two conservationists in India, Ashok Kumar and Belinda Wright, to help him learn more about shahtoosh. Since China had recently declared chiru endangered, buying and selling their wool was forbidden by international law. Many countries would ban the trade if George and his allies could prove that chiru were being slaughtered for shahtoosh.

Sautman, Kumar, and Wright discovered that hundreds of pounds of chiru wool were smuggled into India every year. Indians wove the wool into ultra-fine, ultra-soft, and ultra-expensive shahtoosh shawls. These shawls were sold for thousands of dollars apiece in exclusive shops all over the world. Each fashionable woman wearing a shahtoosh shawl was draping herself with several dead chiru.

The U.S. Fish and Wildlife Service compared samples of shahtoosh shawls to samples of chiru fur under a microscope. They confirmed that shahtoosh did indeed come from chiru. George and other conservationists talked to government officials and journalists, published reports, and sent booklets to politicians, police, wool dealers, and fashion designers around the globe. They told the world the truth about shahtoosh.

Governments warned merchants that shahtoosh was illegal, but some secretly continued to sell it. Police in India, England, France, and the United States raided stores, seized the shawls, and took the shopkeepers to court. A group of wealthy ladies in New York were ordered to turn in shahtoosh shawls they had bought at a charity event. They weren't fined or arrested, but the publicity made many beautiful women realize that wearing shahtoosh was an ugly thing to do.

• • •

AS GEORGE AND OTHER CONSERVATIONISTS campaigned against the shahtoosh trade, China was becoming increasingly aware of the need to protect its remaining wild land and wild animals. On July 19, 1993, the Chinese government officially established the Chang Tang Nature Reserve, an area as large as New Mexico or Germany and eleven times the size of Tanzania's Serengeti National Park. Poachers were tracked down and arrested, and thousands of hides were confiscated and destroyed. In some areas local Tibetans created their own antipoaching patrols.

George scans the Chang Tang for wildlife.

It happened just in time. Poachers had reduced the Chang Tang's chiru population by 90 percent. Out of an estimated one million animals, perhaps only 75,000 remained.

George was grateful for China's protection of the Chang Tang. Yet more needed to be done. His wildlife surveys showed there were at least five main populations of chiru in the Chang Tang, each with its own migration route and calving grounds. Every year the females journeyed to secluded spots to give birth. George suspected that some of these nursery areas lay north of the Chang Tang Nature Reserve's borders. Congregations of chiru would be a tempting target for poachers. If George could trace the migration routes and find the calving grounds, it would be easier for the Chinese government to protect the vulnerable females and their young.

George drove to the top of a hill in the western Chang Tang, near the Aru Basin, and set up his spotting scope. The ring of white mountains on the horizon seemed like the very edge of the world; in the pure, thin air the colors of earth and sky had an almost unreal clarity. A pair of ravens played in the air overhead. George smiled. Ravens carried so many sweet memories: college in Alaska, days in the gorilla forest, the expansive skies of the

Serengeti and the Himalayas. Scattered around his feet were silver-leafed edelweiss, mementos of his childhood in Germany.

George scanned the horizon. A bald hill in the distance appeared to ripple. *Heat wave? Hallucination?* George grabbed his spotting scope. No, it was chiru!

A herd of mothers and fawns several hundred strong flowed over the hill and filled the valley below. Other herds followed. It was like the river of caribou he'd seen as a young man in Alaska.

George built a small blind in the valley by laying flat rocks on edge. He spread himself on the ground, nose in the edelweiss, hoping his scent wouldn't spook the chiru. Part of the herd streamed toward George. From the age of the fawns and the direction the herds were heading, George guessed that the calving grounds must lie to the north, several weeks' walk away. It was one more piece of the puzzle, one more bit of scientific knowledge that could help the chiru.

Female chiru and young. Among other migratory hoofed animals, like caribou and wildebeest, both males and females travel to calving grounds. But among chiru, only the females make the trek. No one knows why only the females migrate.

It was also a scene to warm the spirit. Fawns curled up to rest as their mothers grazed. Hundreds of gentle grunts merged into a comforting murmur, and the fresh scent of crushed grass filled the air. For three hours George was encased within the moving heart of the chiru. Then they traveled on, oblivious to George, the past, and their own uncertain future. The chiru felt only the grass beneath their hooves and the mysterious gravity drawing them toward the far horizon.

To George, this was the essence of the Chang Tang: "Wholeness, stark beauty, and sense of unfettered freedom . . . a place where mind and body can travel, where one's soul can dance."

Chapter 8: The Fate of the Wild

Conservation requires commitment, faith, hope, and a deep moral vision, just as religion does.
— *George B. Schaller*

• • •

George, shown here in Afghanistan, is working to create a transborder International Peace Park that will include parts of Afghanistan, Pakistan, China, and Tajikistan. The park will protect snow leopards, Marco Polo sheep, ibex, brown bears, wolves, and eagles.

GEORGE SCHALLER'S LIFE IN THE WILD has been extraordinarily wide-ranging and productive. In addition to conducting the research described in this book, George studied wild orangutans in Southeast Asia, jaguars and caimans (a kind of alligator) in South America, and brown bears, Bactrian camels, Mongolian gazelle, and snow leopards in Mongolia. A scientific team led by George also rediscovered the Indochinese warty pig—considered extinct for over a hundred years—in a remote corner of Laos. He didn't find this "lost" species while hiking through the jungle, though—he found the pig when a hunter served him one for dinner!

George, now in his seventies, is Vice President of Science and Exploration at the Wildlife Conservation Society. His current fieldwork concentrates on China—as it has for so many years—as well as Afghanistan, Tajikistan, Pakistan, and Iran. When not in the field, he is at home in Connecticut with Kay. Their sons, Eric and Mark, both became scientists. Eric is a biochemist, and Mark is a social psychologist. George and Kay have two grandchildren, Jasper and Maddox.

George now has the pleasure of teaching young scientists and conservationists, just as he himself was once taught by Olaus Murie in Alaska and Doc Emlen in Wisconsin and Africa. "I take students from local universities out into the field," says George. "If they are good, if they are dedicated, we give them money for projects. We have several hundred Wildlife Conservation Society projects in about fifty countries. Almost all are run by local scientists."

Through science, conservation, and education, George continues to work for the protection of the wild creatures and places he has known and loved. This is how they are currently faring.

ALASKA'S GREAT WILDERNESS

The wilderness George studied in 1956 became the Arctic National Wildlife Refuge in 1960. It was enlarged by President Jimmy Carter in 1980. Unfortunately, the 1980 legislation left open the possibility of oil drilling on the coastal plain. For the past thirty years oil companies and politicians have sought permission to drill in the refuge, a proposal George calls "ecological vandalism."

In the summer of 2006, fifty years after his expedition with the Muries, George returned to the Arctic Refuge. He took along two students from the University of Alaska and one from the University of Wyoming. They visited many of the places George had explored in 1956 and camped by the same lake. Mew gulls still nested along the shore, and they found an eagle's nest in the same spot on a limestone cliff. George was heartened to see that the area was as he remembered: a vast, complete ecosystem, pristine and pure. Will we allow it to remain untouched?

THE MOUNTAIN GORILLAS

Seven years after George's landmark study, naturalist Dian Fossey began her own gorilla research in the Virunga Volcanoes. Soon she was working desperately just to keep the gorillas alive. Much of the gorilla forest was turned into farmland, poachers caught infant gorillas for foreign zoos, and adult gorillas were killed so that their heads and hands could be sold as souvenirs. In 1960, George estimated that 450 gorillas lived in the Virunga Volcanoes. By 1972, only about 250 were left. Dian Fossey was murdered in the Virungas in 1985, probably by someone who opposed her antipoaching efforts. Her killer was never found.

The Wildlife Conservation Society helped introduce gorilla tourism in 1978. Tourism fees provide money for conservation, and the presence of tourists makes local people aware of how precious their mountain gorillas are. There are now about 380 mountain gorillas in the Virungas and about 340 in Uganda's Bwindi Impenetrable Forest, a total of 720 animals.

In 1960, George wrote: "All in all, the status of the mountain gorilla is still encouraging, but the total area in which these magnificent apes can be found is small. Constant vigilance must be maintained by conservationists to prevent a disastrous tip of the balance from security to extinction."

The same is true today.

INDIA'S TIGERS

George's study in Kanha National Park brought worldwide attention to the plight of India's wildlife. In 1970, the Indian government banned tiger shooting; three years later, it created Project Tiger to save the majestic predators from extinction. Kanha National Park was named one of the first Project Tiger reserves.

At first, Project Tiger seemed to be succeeding. Villages were moved out of the parks, and regular patrols reduced poaching. Tiger numbers increased. But poaching returned due to the growing demand for tiger bones in Chinese traditional medicine. Hunters kill tigers for their skins, and villagers poison them because the cats kill livestock. The Indian tiger population has once again been reduced to about 1,800 animals. In 2006, the Wildlife Conservation Society and the Panthera Foundation launched Tigers Forever, a new project that hopes to boost tiger populations in a dozen key areas in Asia by 50 percent within ten years.

George revisited Kanha (now called Kanha Tiger Reserve) twenty-five years after his landmark study. He was heartened to see that the park had tripled in size, that villagers had resettled outside, and that wildlife populations had increased dramatically. Today there are about 100 tigers in Kanha; some may be descendants of Cut-Ear and her cubs. Kanha's tigers have plenty to eat, too. Over 20,000 chital roam the meadows. And the park saved the barasingha from extinction; there were only about 75 during George's study, but today Kanha shelters 400 to 500 of the lovely deer.

THE SERENGETI

 George's influential research in Serengeti National Park helped scientists and park wardens better understand predator-prey relations and improved wildlife management around the world.

Yet challenges remain. As Africa's human population has grown, the number of lions has decreased steadily, especially in areas outside parks and reserves. Natural habitat is lost and lions are shot and poisoned for killing domestic livestock. While Tanzania currently has more lions than any other country, its human population has more than tripled since the time of George's study. Control of the disease-carrying tsetse fly has also made it easier for people to live close to Serengeti National Park. Poachers kill an estimated 40,000 to 200,000 Serengeti animals every year. And with more villages near the park, diseases can pass more easily between wild and domestic animals. In 1994 the Serengeti lions were infected with distemper, a disease commonly found in village dogs. One-third of the lions died.

Despite these problems, the Serengeti remains a land of primal power and beauty. Over a million wildebeest, 180,000 Thomson's gazelles, 200,000 zebra, and thousands of impala, buffalo, elephant, topi (a type of antelope), and giraffe roam the plains and woodlands. The lion population recovered from the canine distemper epidemic, and there are now as many lions in the Serengeti as before (about 3,500). A project to vaccinate village dogs will hopefully prevent another outbreak.

Tragically, the Serengeti's wild dogs, with their comic ears and quirky spotted coats, are no more. They were completely wiped out by disease. Small populations survive elsewhere in Tanzania and in a few other African countries.

Snow Leopards of the Himalayas

 "Pen and camera are weapons against oblivion," George wrote. He hoped that his writings and photographs would "induce others to care for the dying mountain world of the Himalaya."

George's pen and camera did make a difference. Shey Phoksumdo National Park, the largest national park in Nepal, was created in 1984. If you want to visit Shey and Crystal Mountain, you still have to walk most of the way.

Khunjerab National Park was established in northern Pakistan in 1975. Today George is working to create a transfrontier park that will include Khunjerab as well as parts of Afghanistan, China, and Tajikistan. This remote, high-altitude wilderness is a sanctuary for snow leopards and rare Marco Polo sheep.

When George left Chitral Gol, Pakistan, he feared protection might come too late to save its wildlife. But in 1984 the area became Chitral Gol National Park. The markhor population has increased sixfold.

In December 2006, scientists captured a female snow leopard in Chitral Gol. She was fitted with a high-tech GPS (global positioning system) satellite collar and released; she is now providing detailed data on snow leopard life. She was named Bayad-e-Kohsaar ("In Memory of Mountains"). Bayad-e-Kohsaar was caught on the same ridge where, thirty-six years earlier, George saw his first snow leopard.

No one is certain how many snow leopards remain, but scientists think there are 200 to 420 in Pakistan and 300 to 500 in Nepal, with a worldwide population of 4,000 to 7,000 scattered across a dozen countries. Unfortunately, in many places snow leopards are still killed for their fur or because they prey on livestock. Snow leopards, like tigers, are also killed to supply bones for traditional Chinese medicine.

China's Pandas

 After George left the Wolong project in 1985, he continued to speak out on behalf of the pandas. He felt he owed it to Zhen-Zhen and the other pandas he had known.

Panda "rescues" lasted until 1987 even though most pandas were not in danger of starvation. A total of 108 pandas were taken into captivity, where many died. Some of the survivors went to breeding centers while others were loaned to foreign zoos. George helped convince zoos to limit their "rent-a-panda" schemes to animals that were not wild-caught and were too old to breed. He also worked to ensure that panda rental fees paid to the Chinese government by foreign zoos were used for wild panda conservation.

Despite early mistakes, China has made a strong and sincere effort to save its pandas. The government banned all logging of natural forests and increased the number of panda reserves from twelve to forty-two. China's panda reserves now have rangers and antipoaching patrols. A recent census found at least 1,600 pandas in the wild. Panda charisma benefits many other rare species, such as musk deer and golden monkeys, that share the panda's misty habitat.

Chinese scientist Pan Wenshi, who worked with George, began his own project in the Qinling Mountains in 1985. For fourteen years Pan Wenshi and his students studied pandas using radio collars and habituation. Habituation is the technique George pioneered with mountain gorillas. George says he takes a "quiet pride" in Pan Wenshi's success.

WILDLIFE OF THE CHANG TANG

Since creating the Chang Tang reserve in 1993, China has established several new protected areas along the borders of the Chang Tang. Together these reserves encompass a vast realm that protects the chiru migration routes and calving grounds.

"Somehow I cannot cease traveling over that sweeping steppe," says George. In 2006, at the age of seventy-three, he made his seventeenth trip to the Chang Tang. With his team of Tibetans and Han Chinese, George drove a thousand miles through the entire northern part of the reserve at altitudes of 16,000 feet and higher. The last traverse of this completely uninhabited area was in 1896, when two British army officers ventured across on horseback.

George's 2006 expedition found that illegal hunting has been greatly reduced, thanks to China's crackdown on poachers and the international effort to end the shahtoosh trade. His most recent wildlife surveys show that chiru, wild yak, and kiang populations are increasing.

The Chang Tang continues to change, and change will bring new challenges. George sees a "new nomadism" as mud-brick huts replace yak-hair tents, motorcycles replace ponies, and fences replace open grazing. More people will put greater pressure on the Chang Tang's scarce resources. Yet the nomads' own conservation work offers hope. Some villages have banned livestock from certain areas to ensure healthy habitat. As a nomad named Gaduo told George: "If the place has wildlife it shows its good condition, and then my family is in good condition also."

These local efforts are deeply satisfying for George. He has long dreamed of making the Chang Tang a haven where wildlife, livestock, and people live in harmony.

ATTITUDES ARE CHANGING. It is heartening that so many people around the world now want to protect their wild places and wild creatures. At the same time, new pressures, problems, and conflicts are unavoidable as the human population—already at six and a half billion—continues to grow.

The world's wildlife needs our help. There is no ultimate victory in conservation, no happy ending that allows us to give a sigh of contentment and close the book. Gorillas, tigers, lions, snow leopards, pandas, and other rare species cannot be permanently "saved." Every generation needs those who can see beyond the lumber value of a redwood, the protein value of a wildebeest, the fashion value of a chiru, and even the entertainment value of a panda. We need young people with the moral vision to grant wild places and wild creatures the right to exist, whole, free, and untouched.

In return we are offered enough beauty to fill our hearts. And for those lucky enough to gaze into the eyes of a wild tiger, we receive wonder, awe—and a lesson in humility.

George's career to date,
by the numbers:

Helped protect over **190,000** square miles of wilderness (an area about the size of Spain)

Took **54,700** photographs

Filled **36,600** notebook pages with data and observations

Wrote **195** scientific and popular articles

Conducted original research in **25** countries

Wrote **16** books

Number of times injured by a wild animal: **0**

Getting Involved

• "Every one of our acts is an ecological act," says George. "Drink a Coke and the sugar was grown somewhere and transported, the water pumped using electricity, the aluminum can mined and manufactured." Most of what we do uses energy—and our energy use is fueling global warming. Global warming is the most important conservation problem of our time, because it threatens species and habitats everywhere on Earth. All of us can promote conservation by using less energy.

• Spreading the word is important. Talk to your family and friends about conservation, and write to politicians and policymakers to urge them to protect wild animals and wild lands.

• Many conservation groups have very little money and are very grateful for help with fund-raising. Contact an organization that appeals to you and ask how you can help. A bake sale or car wash is also an opportunity to educate others about conservation.

• Hands-on experience is invaluable. Is there an endangered animal living nearby, or a patch of wilderness someone is trying to preserve? Is there a nature club at your school? Read your newspaper to learn more about local conservation issues, or contact a local chapter of a national organization like the Sierra Club, the Audubon Society, or the National Wildlife Federation.

• Take the initiative. You may know of a problem no one else has noticed, such as a trash-clogged stream. Create your own conservation project, perhaps with the help of an interested teacher, and enlist others to help. As the scientist Margaret Mead once said, "Never doubt that a small group of thoughtful, committed citizens can change the world. Indeed, it is the only thing that ever has."

Internet and Multimedia Resources

INTERNET

The Wildlife Conservation Society (www.wcs.org), where George Schaller is Vice President of Science and Exploration, provides information about George's current projects and the endangered animals discussed in this book. WCS also has a special Teens for Planet Earth site at www.teensforplanetearth.org

You can tag along with Alaska's caribou and find information on Arctic ecology at www.taiga.net; check out the Porcupine Caribou Herd Satellite Collar Project.

The Mountain Gorilla Veterinary Project is actively involved in protecting gorillas. Go to http://mgvp.32ad.com to learn more.

Dr. Craig Packer of the University of Minnesota has studied the Serengeti's lions for three decades; some of the animals are descendants of the lions George knew in the 1960s. Dr. Packer's Lion Research Center (www.lionresearch.org) has a wealth of information on lions, including Project Lifelion, an ongoing effort to protect the wild carnivores of the Serengeti from the diseases of domestic dogs.

You can find information on snow leopard conservation on the websites of the Snow Leopard Trust (www.snowleopard.org) and the Snow Leopard Conservancy (www.snowleopardconservancy.org).

WWF (www.panda.org) remains involved in panda conservation in China, and Conservation International (www.conservation.org) is embarking on a major new panda conservation project.

MULTIMEDIA

Champions of the Wild: Mountain Gorillas. Omni Film Productions, 2000. This documentary chronicles a return visit by George to the Virunga Volcanoes.

Mountain Gorilla. National Geographic IMAX movie, Warner Home Video, 1991. George and Kay Schaller appear briefly in this film, which includes excellent footage of mountain gorillas.

Mountains of the Snow Leopard. Survival Anglia, 1994. This documentary describes George's research in Mongolia.

Planet Earth. BBC Warner, 2007. Of particular interest are the episodes "From Pole to Pole" (African wild dogs); "Mountains" (snow leopards, markhor, pandas, golden monkeys, musk deer); "Great Plains" (caribou, wild yak, wild asses, lions); "Deserts" (lions); "Seasonal Forests" (tigers, chital, gaur); "Saving Species" (snow leopards, tigers); "Into the Wilderness" (caribou, wild dogs); and "Living Together" (lions, markhor, snow leopards).

Save the Panda. National Geographic Society, Washington, D.C., 1983. This film chronicles the early days of the panda project, including footage of George and Kay Schaller in the field.

Silent Roar: Searching for the Snow Leopard. Nature Video Library, Thirteen/WNET New York and Wild Wise Ltd., 2005. This video offers rare footage of snow leopards in the wild.

George and Martin Robards, a student at the University of Alaska, Fairbanks, compare photos of the 1956 Murie expedition campsite with the same site fifty years later.

Sources

This book could not have been written without the generous assistance of George and Kay Schaller. George spent many hours with me, patiently answering questions and sharing photographs and excerpts from his field notes. Kay contributed her own memories, anecdotes, and perspective. Both spent many hours correcting and commenting on drafts of this text, including reviewing all statements attributed to them.

Print resources recommended for a general audience are marked with an asterisk (*).

GENERAL SOURCES

*Schaller, George. *A Naturalist and Other Beasts.* San Francisco: Sierra Club Books, 2007.

CHAPTER 1: THE CALL OF THE WILD

*Banerjee, Subhankar. *Arctic National Wildlife Refuge: Seasons of Life and Land.* Seattle: Mountaineers Books, 2003.
Kaye, Roger. *Last Great Wilderness: The Campaign to Establish the Arctic National Wildlife Refuge.* Fairbanks: University of Alaska Press, 2006.
*Murie, Margaret E. *Two in the Far North.* New York: Alfred A. Knopf, 1962.

Quotes on page 10: "Grizzlies!" (Murie, p. 332); page 11: "From the top" (Murie, p. 343); page 13: "I guess it's time" (Murie, p. 435).

CHAPTER 2: GORILLA FOREST

Akeley, Carl E. *In Brightest Africa.* Garden City: Doubleday, Page and Company, 1923.
Du Chaillu, Paul B. *Explorations and Adventures in Equatorial Africa.* London: John Murray, 1861.
Schaller, George. *The Mountain Gorilla.* Chicago: University of Chicago Press, 1963.
*Schaller, George. *The Year of the Gorilla.* Chicago: University of Chicago Press, 1964

Quotes on page 15: "Then the underbrush swayed" (Du Chaillu, pp. 70–71); page 16: "The white man" (Akeley, p. 196).

CHAPTER 3: A CLAN OF TIGERS

Schaller, George. *The Deer and the Tiger.* Chicago: University of Chicago Press, 1967.
*Schaller, George. "My Year with the Tigers." *Life Magazine,* June 25, 1965, pp. 60–66.

Quote on page 27: "The Striped One" (Rudyard Kipling, *The Jungle Books,* Signet Classics, New York, 2005, p. 173).

CHAPTER 4: LION COUNTRY

*Schaller, George. *Golden Shadows, Flying Hooves*. New York: Alfred A. Knopf, 1973.
*Schaller, George. "Life with the King of Beasts." *National Geographic*, April 1969, pp. 494–519.
*Schaller, George. *Serengeti: A Kingdom of Predators*. New York: Alfred A. Knopf, 1972.
Schaller, George. *The Serengeti Lion: A Study of Predator–Prey Relations*. Chicago: University of Chicago Press, 1972.

Quotes on pages 39–40: "Our dual past" (Schaller, *Serengeti: A Kingdom of Predators*, p. ix).

CHAPTER 5: CAT AMONG THE CLOUDS

Hedin, Sven. *Central Asia and Tibet*. London: Hurst and Blackett, 1903.
*Matthiessen, Peter. *The Snow Leopard*. New York: Viking Press, 1978.
Schaller, George. *Mountain Monarchs: Wild Sheep and Goats of the Himalaya*. Chicago: University of Chicago Press, 1977.
*Schaller, George. *Stones of Silence*. New York: Viking Press, 1979.

Quotes on page 58: "the gigantic wall" (Hedin, p. 33); "I wish we were up" (Matthiessen, p. 28); page 59: "[If it] were not" (Matthiessen, p. 25); "This is the first" (Matthiessen, p. 150); page 61: "Isn't that something" (Matthiessen, p. 221).

CHAPTER 6: PANDA POLITICS

*Lu Zhi. *Giant Pandas in the Wild*. New York: Aperture, 2002.
*Schaller, George. *The Last Panda*. Chicago: University of Chicago Press, 1993.
Schaller, George, with Hu Junchu, Pan Wenshi, and Zhu Jing. *The Giant Pandas of Wolong*. Chicago: University of Chicago Press, 1985.

CHAPTER 7: ASSES AND ANTELOPES

Hedin, Sven. *Central Asia and Tibet*. London: Hurst and Blackett, 1903.
Hedin, Sven. *My Life as an Explorer*. Washington, D.C.: National Geographic Adventure Classics, 2003 (first published 1925).
*Ridgeway, Rick. *The Big Open: On Foot Across Tibet's Chang Tang*. Washington, D.C.: National Geographic Society, 2004.
*Schaller, George. "In a High and Sacred Realm." *National Geographic*, August 1993, pp. 63–87.
*Schaller, George. *Tibet's Hidden Wilderness*. New York: Harry N. Abrams, 1997.
Schaller, George. *Wildlife of the Tibetan Steppe*. Chicago: University of Chicago Press, 1998.

Quotes on page 77: "All distances" (Hedin, *Central Asia*, p. 514); page 80: "It is hard" (Hedin, *My Life*, p. 257).

CHAPTER 8: THE FATE OF THE WILD

*Fossey, Dian. *Gorillas in the Mist*. Boston: Houghton Mifflin, 1983.
*Hillard, Darla. *Vanishing Tracks: Four Years Among the Snow Leopards of Nepal*. New York: Arbor House, 1989.

*Karanth, K. Ullas. *The Way of the Tiger: Natural History and Conservation of the Endangered Big Cat.* Vancouver: Voyageur Press, 2001.

Moulton, Carroll. *Kanha Tiger Reserve: Portrait of an Indian National Park.* Mumbai: Vakils, Feffer and Simons Ltd., 1999.

*Packer, Craig. *Into Africa.* Chicago: University of Chicago Press, 1994.

*Schaller, George. "The Mountain Gorilla." *New Scientist*, January 4, 1962.

*Schaller, George. "Reflections in a Hidden Land" (essay). In *Himalaya: Personal Stories of Grandeur, Challenge, and Hope*, edited by Richard C. Blum, Erica Stone, and Broughton Coburn. Washington, D.C.: National Geographic Society, 2006.

*Schaller, George, and Michael Nichols. *Gorilla: Struggle for Survival in the Virungas.* New York: Aperture, 1988.

*Thapar, Valmik. *Tiger: The Ultimate Guide.* New York: CDS Books, 2004.

*Weber, Bill, and Amy Vedder. *In the Kingdom of Gorillas: Fragile Species in a Dangerous Land.* New York: Simon and Schuster, 2001.

Quotes on page 87: "Conservation requires" (Schaller, "Reflections," p. 148); page 89: "All in all, the status" (Schaller, "The Mountain Gorilla," p. 18).

Acknowledgments

In writing this book, I have had the great privilege of getting to know George and Kay Schaller. Both read over multiple drafts of the text and generously opened their home to me while I conducted interviews and searched through George's image collection for just the right photos. Their kindness and patience are much appreciated. In honor of all they have done to help wildlife, I am donating my royalties from this book to the Wildlife Conservation Society for projects designated by George.

Several years ago, when I found myself in tears at the end of Phillip Hoose's wonderful book *The Race to Save the Lord God Bird*, I knew I had found the right editor and publisher for *A Life in the Wild*. Melanie Kroupa understood my vision for this book from the very beginning and shepherded it through to the very end. I am deeply grateful to her and the Farrar, Straus and Giroux team, including Jay Colvin and Karla Reganold. I am also indebted to my agent, Caryn Wiseman, for her sage advice, and to Beth Wald for generously allowing me to use a wonderful photo of George in the field.

On the home front, I am very grateful to my husband, Rob Townsend, for his constant support and encouragement. Thanks also to my three children, Travis, Kelsey, and Connor, for coping with my occasional physical and frequent mental absences. My critique partners—Carol Peterson, Keely Parrack, Deborah Underwood, and Nancy Humphrey Case—gave detailed feedback on multiple versions of this manuscript and provided a steady flow of reassurance.

The reader might suspect that writing about close encounters between George and various wild animals would be difficult, since I was obviously not present. Those parts were surprisingly easy to re-create. For that I would like to thank, among others, a mountain gorilla in Rwanda, a nurse shark off New Guinea, a ring-tailed mongoose in Madagascar, a hyena in Tanzania, and a giant manta ray off Costa Rica. You gave me not only inspiration for this book but also some of the most wondrous moments of my life.

Index

George with a young white-lipped peccary (a kind of wild pig). George kept the peccary as a pet while he was studying jaguars in Brazil.